"I have watched the growth and development of David's ideas working with the very best run companies in the world."

—Jack Goldsmith, Co-founder, MARC

"Since my first opportunity to work with David Shaner at Frito-Lay, I have become a convinced follower of the techniques detailed in *The Seven Arts of Change*."

—John "Jack" V. Rice, PhD, Senior Vice President, W.I.N.G.S. Inc.;
Former Director of Training and Development, Frito-Lay

"*The Seven Arts* influenced my life deeply. Under David Shaner's guidance, my career took off and I discovered for myself the benefits of true mind and body coordination. I highly recommend this book for anyone interested in improving their performance and thus actualizing their true potential."

—Tony Stevenson, Principal Soloist, Metropolitan Opera

"So compelling, so applicable."

—Greg Gardner, SuccessFactors, Inc.

"As someone with decades of experience in human resources in a large corporation, I appreciate the practical yet profound wisdom David's Seven Arts offer. I highly recommend this read."

—James E. Eubanks, Human Resources Executive,
Global Card Services, Bank of America

"The Seven Arts can help you and your organization live a healthier, more prosperous life."

—Thomas Crum, Author of *Three Deep Breaths, Journey to Center,* and
The Magic of Conflict; Founder and President, Aiki Works Inc.

The Seven Arts of Change

Leading Business Transformation That Lasts

David Shaner

UNION SQUARE PRESS
An imprint of Sterling Publishing Co., Inc.

New York / London
www.sterlingpublishing.com

STERLING and the distinctive Sterling logo are registered trademarks of
Sterling Publishing Co., Inc.

Library of Congress Cataloging-in-Publication Data
Shaner, David.
The seven arts of change : leading business transformation that lasts / David Shaner.
p. cm.
ISBN 978-1-4027-6784-5
1. Organizational change. 2. Success in business. I. Title.
HD58.8.S476 2010
658.4'06--dc22

2010016938

2 4 6 8 10 9 7 5 3 1

Published by Sterling Publishing Co., Inc.
387 Park Avenue South, New York, NY 10016
© 2010 by David Shaner
Distributed in Canada by Sterling Publishing
^c/o Canadian Manda Group, 165 Dufferin Street
Toronto, Ontario, Canada M6K 3H6
Distributed in the United Kingdom by GMC Distribution Services
Castle Place, 166 High Street, Lewes, East Sussex, England BN7 1XU
Distributed in Australia by Capricorn Link (Australia) Pty. Ltd.
P.O. Box 704, Windsor, NSW 2756, Australia

Sterling ISBN 978-1-4027-6784-5

For information about custom editions, special sales, premium and
corporate purchases, please contact Sterling Special Sales
Department at 800-805-5489 or specialsales@sterlingpublishing.com.

Dedication

This book is dedicated to all the employees who first actively participated, then acted responsibly, then executed the business plan, and then extended the benefits across the value chain (from suppliers to customers). Most importantly, I am grateful to each and every one of you for taking a risk and helping this Seven Arts vision become a reality. It has been my hope from the beginning that these Arts might be of personal benefit to you extended even more fully beyond the workplace. This is the fullest extension, and most meaningful extension, of the inclusive Seven Arts process. I hope that the quality of not only your work life, but also your personal life and spiritual life, has been positively affected by our shared learning and experience. I thank you for your trust, openness, and willingness to put yourself in the place of your partner. Remember that your life itself is your true monastery. And, since much of your life is spent working, why not let work itself become your whetstone for true spiritual transformation.

Contents

Introduction

Why a spiritual guide for change? Because the big meeting often goes like this:

The leader expresses his belief in the organization. All that ability, he says, is needed now because the firm is facing extraordinary challenges. The economy, overseas competition, and [insert your own hurdles here] have mounted enormous pressure on the company, and, as a result, numbers are down and quality is slipping. Change needs to happen yesterday.

To meet the new challenges, the best and brightest consulting firm on the planet has reviewed the situation and blessed the company with their five-step prescription to thrive in today's market. Via a company-wide presentation, the leader "PowerPoints" the magic initiatives. Now, he concludes, it is up to everyone to team up and dig in. The organization is going to make it! Employees walk out with a sense of urgency and vitality that might last the afternoon. For the moment, they believe they won't lose their jobs.

The following day, everything settles to the status quo. The sparks of urgency and vigor dim. Some employees realize they don't understand the new plans and are frustrated. A few resent that outsiders dictated the plan of action. Others are apathetic. The unified vision of change begins unraveling, one emotion, one action at a time.

And so this is the progression of the common story: The leader expresses the need for change. The people don't buy it, get it, or care about it. And the change never happens.

Changing How You Change

Nearly every study of organizational change over the past two decades indicates that companies fail to make the change they intend approximately 70 percent of the time. And so the question forever being raised is: Why do change initiatives flop far more often than they fly? Volumes are written on the subject every year. Yet, most don't answer the question correctly, if at all. Allow me to put this rub to rest right away:

Change efforts fail when the spirit of a company remains the same.

A leader might be right about everything—the need to change, the reasons for change, and the timing of change. He might be extremely convincing in his pep talk. But if the leader doesn't understand where change begins, change won't happen, no matter how urgent it is.

Before organizational change can succeed, it must first occur at the subtle spiritual level in the individuals of the organization. That's because the spirit is the foundational source of energy that runs through our bodies and gives our lives meaning. Your spirit is the sum of your beliefs, your convictions, your moral codes and standards. All lasting transformation must begin there because, ultimately, your spirit and mine is the primary driver of all our behavior.

Without grounding at the spiritual level, the change process becomes a cooked-up breadbasket of external tactics that never takes hold. Employees might do as they're told for a time, but they will eventually default to the behaviors driven by their spirits. In short, without tapping into the defaults of organizational behavior, people's behavior remains the same. It always has and always will.

I tell you this with a high degree of certainty because I've stood in the midst of change efforts for three decades. In one area of my life, I have helped professional athletes and artists transition to world-class performers. In another area, I transformed myself to top levels in both athletics and academics. In another area, I have helped massive organizations such as Umbro, Frito-Lay, Ryobi, Duracell, Gillette, and Owens Corning Composites achieve their change goals with a 100 percent success rate. All this change succeeded because it started at the spiritual level first.

But I didn't see this right away. I used to differentiate each activity from the others, not seeing the underlying connections beneath them all.

Looking back, I can see now that I probably didn't link my diverse personal experiences of change with my change guidance because I was concerned my clients—particularly my corporate clients—would think me too unconventional. I figured that in a time when change was urgent, they'd be looking for decisive action and strong leadership, not personal development philosophy.

And so, when I worked with a well-known tenor from the Metropolitan Opera, I packaged my guidance into the context of music metaphors and theory—even though it was based on my lifelong practice of *Ki-Aikido* and the mindset I developed as a competitive downhill skier. When I worked with large international corporations like Mitsubishi Chemical, I translated my guidance into the cross-cultural business vernacular of goal setting, bottom lines, and shareholder value. I never considered mentioning that I'd learned many of these lessons as a professor of philosophy and Asian studies, or from my unique experience serving as a deputy sheriff in Aspen, Colorado—even though these things were inextricably linked to what I was teaching them. I assumed clients would wonder, *Who is this snow-bum/ philosopher/kung-fu fighter with no grasp of business reality?* I assumed I would lose them at the first hint of spirituality or ancient thought.

I have since learned my assumptions were dead wrong.

When I finally began to let the cat out of the bag and divulge to my clients the real foundation beneath my unique change guidance, I discovered that individuals and organizations alike responded with dramatic results to what I now call the Seven Arts approach to change. At its core, it is a spiritual guide to change that works whether you are changing a sports franchise, a mom-'n'-pop shop, a corporate conglomerate, or yourself.

I should have known my clients would respond well to knowing the spiritual truth behind the curtain of my guidance, as the same spiritual truths allowed me to navigate what appears to be an implausible journey of change in my own life—a journey that led to seemingly disparate expertise in downhill ski racing, martial arts, academia, and business.

I'll share the details of these diverse experiences in the coming pages, but, for now, it's important that you understand where this spiritual guide for change came from.

As a child, I was curious about everything different. Anything my parents would not or could not explain was immediately elevated in my mind as something exotic, something to be remembered, explored, and, ultimately, understood. My subsequent journeys led me to a love of unconventional wisdom. When I came across something that sparked my sacred curiosity, I jumped headlong into learning everything I could about it. I didn't always seek to become the best in that field, but I did always seek to learn from the best. This gave me an incredibly unique and behind-the-scenes understanding of several disciplines. (In fact, I actually lived with my highly acclaimed teachers in two different instances.)

From my teenage years, my life wound from learning competitive downhill skiing from a world-class coach named Jean-Pierre Pascal and a downhill champion named Philippe Mollard . . . to studying *Aikido* under Master Koichi Tohei, the man who brought the martial art from Japan to the United States in 1953, . . . to studying Asian philosophy under the world's foremost authorities in Hawaii . . . to understanding the biological basis of behavior from Harvard's Stephen Jay Gould and Edward O. Wilson . . . to learning about law enforcement as a deputy under Dick Kienast, the famous sheriff of Pitkin County, Colorado, . . . to then applying my diverse education in contexts as far-ranging as a Fulbright Project serving Prime Minister Indira Gandhi, to peak performance sessions for National Football League (NFL) and National Hockey League (NHL) players, to a thirteen-year change initiative for Duracell.

My love of "different" wisdom was not actually leading me down the path of a pinball as it seemed. Instead, the knowledge became a snowball, growing in size and scope as I rolled around every turn. This wisdom I was gathering was accumulating into something much more significant than a nice metaphorical lesson here and there.

Now here's where I should stop and admit something: I didn't see this snowball until I sat down six years ago to finish the last chapter of a sort of self-help memoir I was writing about personal and spiritual development based on the things I'd learned from my various mentors. While I had successfully led numerous companies through change initiatives at that point, I couldn't give a concrete answer about why I'd been so successful. I still felt as though I had been winging it. It wasn't until I was sitting outside at the picnic table in my backyard garden, penning the last sentence of my memoir that it hit me: Could it be that this seven-part path to individual spiritual development was the same path I had been using to guide organizations through change initiatives for many, many years?

Yes, I said to myself. It's all right here. The phrasing was different but the elements of successful change were precisely the same. Each Art for personal spiritual development had a precise counterpart in the process of organizational change I had been using all these years.

The realization hit me with such clarity that I immediately set out to write a new book—this book. This time I would write a book focused upon successful change management and business development based upon my three decades of consulting experience; first, with the Alexander Proudfoot Company, and second, with my own company starting nearly twenty-five years ago.

* * *

In the following seven chapters, you will discover, as I did, that by following seven basic Arts of spiritual development, you will be highly successful at not only leading change, but also sustaining change throughout an organization. Here briefly are those Seven Arts and the primary actions that embody each one:

THE SEVEN ARTS FOR SUCCESSFUL CHANGE

1. The Art of Preparation: Assessment

2. The Art of Compassion: Participation

3. The Art of Responsibility: Accountability

4. The Art of Relaxation: Clarity, Focus, Visibility

5. The Art of Conscious Action: Execution

6. The Art of Working Naturally: Sustainability

7. The Art of Service: Generosity

These Seven Arts are the fundamental elements of any change process because they go to the most basic level of human behavior, the spirit.

I should warn you that by "fundamental" and "basic," I do not mean they are easy or quick to accomplish. If you want a superficial method to coerce change out of yourself or your organization, you won't find it in these pages. As I tell my *Ki-Aikido* students, the Seven Arts will be demanding, but they will be the most exhilarating and valuable thing you can ever do.

WHY THE ARTS WORK

This book is written to those in positions that require them to lead change for departments, teams, and organizations of various sizes. But there is no rule that says you have to be in a position of leadership to lead change. Every one of us is a change leader in our own lives, first and foremost. And the truth is that it is only when we can effectively change ourselves that we can be effective in changing the lives of others. This book will serve you in both regards.

Whether your goal is to combine corporate cultures following a merger or to revamp a nonprofit to fit with the times, you will always achieve the best results by turning to spiritual principles at each phase of the process. In this way, you will at once be promoting both individual growth and team chemistry as each member is held together and motivated from the same foundation.

I use this strategy with all of my clients, and the results are undeniable. For example, my change guidance at Duracell (from 1987 to 2000) helped to yield a 2,000 percent increase in shareholder value, a 650 percent increase in revenue, a 24 percent per-year compounded increase in gross alkaline unit sales, a 400-plus percent improvement in operational efficiencies, and the purchase of the company by Gillette in 1996 for $7.82 billion.

The Seven Arts are so effective because they allow an organization to decisively answer questions about its future in the most fundamentally sound manner—at the spiritual level. This is key, because failing to answer the key questions correctly—if at all—is the one common thread among failed initiatives. People are either left in the dark or they never grasp the change on a personal level. The Seven Arts avoid this fate because they require your organization to approach change on a spiritual level so the people become unified at their core, enabling your culture to change at its deepest foundation.

Ultimately, to change the collective spirit of an organization's people is to change its culture. You'll recall I previously asserted that change efforts fail because those leading the effort fail to facilitate a change in the spirit of the organization. That is to say, change fails when the spiritual roots of the culture stay the same.

My interchanging use of the terms *spirit* and *culture* is deliberate and has an important point. The term *culture* has become like old chewing gum; it has lost its flavor from years of overjawing. As a result, we don't quite know what we mean when we say "organizational culture." It means different things to different people in different circumstances. Let's avoid this cloudiness altogether.

The term *spirit* points to the foundational humanity—the human spirit—from which all organizational achievement springs. This is organizational culture at its core: people believing, behaving, and expecting in a collective manner. At times, this collective humanity is wilted or collectively stifled. At other times, it is spry and collectively progressive. This spiritual characterization of culture is critical for you to understand as the leader because the majority of your competition (and, frankly, organizations in general) characterize their culture superficially. This is an unreliable foundation from which to lead change because it does not account for the core drivers behind all organizational activity.

The bottom line is that, despite how technological and automated organizations have become, at their core they remain a collection of human energies that are merely being applied in an organized environment. Resurrecting and guiding that human core of your organization is the secret to leading and sustaining change.

For this reason, I will refer to your organization's culture as its spirit, and vice versa. I will use the terms interchangeably so that this important paradigm shift happens more naturally over the course of the reading. In the end, the new vernacular will become your own, along with the process of lasting organizational change.

WHERE? WHAT? WHOSE? HOW? WHEN? WHY? THE ANSWERS UNDERLYING ORGANIZATIONAL CHANGE

Before I enter into a change initiative with any organization, I explain the six primary questions that must be answered to give the leaders context for making spiritual change. It is important we do the same here. Think of the questions as the canvas on which your organization will apply the Arts. Answering the six questions prepares your canvas for change. Applying the Seven Arts is your change masterpiece. Here first, are the questions you will learn to answer successfully:

Primary Question #1: Where is the organization's culture?

Change management initiatives often false-start when the leader cannot or does not answer this question. In fact, answering the question is so critical that I ask change leaders to answer it right away, and I keep asking until they arrive at the answer.

"Where is the culture of your business?" I ask. "Is the culture in the building? The equipment? Is it in the intellectual property? In the brands you own?"

"No," everyone says. "The culture is in our people."

They then look at me expecting confirmation.

"Okay," I reply, "but where in the people is the culture?"

Eventually, we get to the fact that the culture is in people's hearts and heads. It is not tangible. Culture is the sum total of the emotions, experiences, beliefs, and expectations of everyone involved with the organization. I call this sum total the *collective mind* of the organization.

Whether your organization is made up of five people or fifty thousand, your culture is created and sustained in the sum total of what each person thinks, believes, feels, and expects about the organization. Nothing will change in the organization's culture until you figure out how to change that collective mind of your organization.

Occasionally, leaders have a major crisis on their hands and ask me, "How fast can we change the culture?"

"In a day," I tell them.

"You can?" is their astonished response.

"Yes," I say, "but the only way to do this is to fire 100 percent of your people. Do that and you empty the organization's mind; from there you can fill it with whatever culture you desire."

Since this is a ludicrous option for most, changing the spirit of an organization typically begins as an exercise in understanding. You must be able to characterize your organization's collective mind. What are its core emotions, experiences, beliefs, and expectations? Until you can describe these things, you cannot change the spirit. That's because you cannot motivate people to change their behavior without understanding their motives for speaking and acting.

Perhaps you can now see why changing an organization is so difficult. Its main ingredients are not tangible. You cannot see the collective mind that dictates the activity of your culture. But you can clearly measure behavior and, therefore, glean clear evidence of what's in the collective mind of any organization.

Suffice it to say for now that, if you are a leader, you must know what defines your people's predominant behavior—and this requires knowing where to look. At the end of the day, all resistance to organizational change begins in your organization's collective mind. Unless you develop a strategy for changing things there, your change efforts will not be understood, accepted, or executed.

I cannot overstate this point, because it is the foundation to everything else you will learn. That which hinders a company from changing is ultimately inside the people. It is the collective voice that says, "Is this really necessary?" or, "We'll get to that later," or, "Let's keep that in mind." You must uncover, comprehend, and acknowledge these objections, or no change effort will take hold. You must answer, "Where is the culture?" with confidence to know what sort of change must occur. Answering the question will inform you of an accurate baseline for change. By first understanding the collective mind of your organization, you establish a place from which you can effectively birth the change process.

Primary Question #2: What starts the process?

The tendency is to assume action is required to begin the change process. The truth is that that's much further down the road. The company that jumps into action for action's sake acts on unsubstantiated whim. Such action rarely results in lasting change.

The one thing that starts every process of successful change is knowledge. Without it, employees, managers, and executives cannot participate effectively in altering the direction of the organization. While this is a very basic concept, few leaders help employees understand the real business environment. This includes understanding the reality of new overseas competition, the reality of new technologies, and the reality of industry consolidation or expansion that dramatically affects the bottom line. I call this significant educational effort providing "boardroom awareness" to every employee.

In decades of working with senior executives and corporate boards, I have yet to learn anything so difficult that I could not explain it to a person with an eighth-grade education. (For example, you can explain the effective management of significant debt after a leveraged buyout simply by equating the issue with paying interest on money you borrowed to purchase a car.) Yet, "it's too complicated" is a common excuse.

The only theory necessary to sustain a healthy business surrounds two basic concepts: (1) "Buy low, sell high" (unless you're "shorting" the market), and (2) "Profit is revenue, less cost." That's it. The execution of a good strategy, however, is not so easy because the executors are people with emotions, habits, beliefs, and expectations that must be in sync with the business plan at the deepest level. Getting people there is a complex task, but it begins with a solid understanding of the business they are being asked to change.

Employees need to know the environment in which the change process is being executed. And as much as possible, they need to know the visible metrics being used to keep score so they can gauge if their collective mind is on target. Mind leads behavior. Your organization's intelligence—the collective knowledge of its collective mind—is its truest value. If you misjudge or guess at this, you will always struggle to lead change.

Primary Question #3: Whose culture is it?

Change requires that you help everyone take personal responsibility for his or her role in necessary transformation. Your people must believe the culture is theirs to own. If you want people to think and act like an owner, the concept of "owning" the work environment must be clear.

In order to give your people a sense of ownership for the success of the enterprise, you must create tangible ways for them to participate in the change process. Without meaningful, heartfelt participation, people will not take responsibility for the improvement (or survival) of the organization. In most workplaces, people do not perform to the very best of their ability simply because they do not care.

To create lasting change, you must attach a deeper purpose to the work they do. When there is personal, spiritual meaning attached to your people's work, they care enough to work harder or in a different manner.

Work must become reinterpreted in the collective mind of the participants of change. It must become known as a place for personal growth, achievement, satisfaction, and spiritual development. If your people learn how to (1) exercise their potential, (2) reach new performance heights, (3) develop interpersonal skills, and (4) improve their ability to collaborate with a diversity of people, then the entire change process becomes an opportunity to expand personal awareness, creativity, tolerance, and fulfillment.

Primary Question #4: "How do you know if you are making progress?"

Since the culture of your organization exists in its collective mind and this mind is not tangible, you must focus on visible behaviors. It is one thing to say you are going to change (for example, lose weight, work out, stop smoking, or do more community service), but it is quite another thing to actually change your behavior.

Are your people walking the talk? As the leader of this process, you must learn to not only read the invisible mind of the organization, you must read visible changes in speech, action, and regular behavior that signify the change initiative is taking place effectively. When you see change in your organization's collective behavior, you know change in the collective mind is taking place.

Primary Question #5: "When can you change the culture?"

People involved in a change process must challenge their previous ways of thinking and behaving. Those old habits have, in part, led to the present crisis the organization is addressing. Unfortunately, most think they can wait to change. They do not realize how much the change process is held back by their habitual ways of thinking and behaving—by the ways they have traditionally perceived themselves and their role, responsibility, and relationship to the organization.

As the leader, it is your job to guide your people to think and act in the present moment instead of according to their collective memory of the past. The way you have always done things exists in the collective memory of your organization. This includes the sum total of past emotions, experiences, and expectations of each employee, customer, supplier, and shareholder. This institutional memory can be toxic.

The only time when you can change the spirit of your organization is right now. World-class athletes know this. They unwaveringly focus on daily goals and improvement because the present moment is the only time they can (and do) improve. In the same way, leaders of change must create a sense of urgency because they understand successful execution will require that people do not wait to change themselves. Everyone must be coached to think and act differently—now.

A negative institutional memory will be the primary deterrent to people changing today. Some of these attached thoughts include "That's the way we have always done things," or, "Let's wait for others to change," or, "Let's wait for our supervisor to get on board." These institutionalized mantras hold people back. They become the equivalent of an organizational emergency brake, hindering all progress. They are the root cause of the 70 percent failure rate of change initiatives.

So, when can you change the culture? The answer is *now*. But you can't just say it. Instead, you must lead people's thinking and behavior. Bad habits are old habits, and they exist first inside a person's head. Changing how the collective mind functions today is the key to removing dependency on old habits.

The Seven Arts to be discussed in this book construct a paradigm that recognizes leading change initiatives requires everyone to feel, think, and behave in ways that address the present needs and opportunities, not in ways that support memories of the past.

Primary Question #6: "Why do people change?"

The need to change is usually met with resistance. Most people value predictability, even if it's predictable mediocrity. If the leader of change cannot offer a consistent and compelling rationale for change, he will fail to win the collective mind of the organization, and change will not happen.

The compelling reason for change must not only be due to the urgent business crisis. It must also include a commitment to support and enable each individual to grow and develop personally. Your workplace must become a vehicle for desirable personal growth and development, and it must be understood as such in the collective mind.

When people begin to trust senior management, when they are meaningfully included in the direction of the business, when they participate in the rewards that accompany superior achievement, then you will have an organization where the people know why they are giving 120 percent.

Why do people change? They change because they are given a clear reason to.

PUTTING IT ALL TOGETHER

By canvassing the six questions over your organization and then painting the Seven Arts atop them, you will be able to lead your people to a deeper, more meaningful level of change in their own lives. You will be putting personal emotions, personal growth, and personal experience before the organization's needs. By doing so, you will possess the ability to effectively lead the organization—a collection of individuals—to change in the new direction it needs to succeed.

By applying the Seven Arts, you will essentially be doing unto others as you would have them do unto you. You will learn in the process that the Golden Rule is not merely good spiritual practice; it is also a principled way to effectively lead and motivate others. Employing the Seven Arts inspires positive change because you, the leader, are guiding meaningful, organizational improvement that ultimately benefits every individual employee. I will show you precisely what that looks like in the coming pages.

As with any spiritual practice, putting your positive insights to work requires more than words. Translating the necessary answers we've just discussed into strategic, proven action is the focus of the Seven Arts. Specifically, you will learn how to serve and develop others so they can serve and develop the organization. This is the irrefutable link between spiritual development and leading successful change. Both require strong, trustworthy guidance at the deepest human level.

* * *

As I finally discovered for myself, it is no coincidence that this mixture of leadership strategy and spiritual development works. It's something that I always innately knew and used to guide me, even if I didn't consciously know I was doing it. I have always believed that treating people well and having a better business go hand in hand.

Each chapter of the book will cover one of the Seven Arts. I will describe how it came to be a fixture in my strategy for organizational change and why it matters. We will then examine separately how it relates to and can be practiced by your organization. I'll provide many examples from both my corporate and individual performance consulting to give the Arts handles for you to pick up and apply to your own specific circumstances.

But I must remind you that these are "Arts," not sciences. The application of them requires your own unique treatment. Because the culture and makeup of every company is different, I cannot give you an exact prescription for successfully leading change in your organization. Any author who tells you he can is blowing smoke.

What I can and will do now is get you at the right pharmacy (spirituality) and in the right aisle (the human spirit) to discover your prescription for effective change. Once you possess the remedy for overcoming resistance to change, you will see clearly how successful change can occur in your personal life as well as in your organization.

THE ART OF PREPARATION

DURING THE SUMMER OF 1982, I had an experience that solidified my thoughts about the initial requirements of widespread change. In this case, the desired change was far broader than in an organization; the change was to take place over the entire country of India.

After accepting a professorship at Furman University in Greenville, South Carolina, one of my first responsibilities was to travel to India as part of a Fulbright Fellowship. (I was chosen for the opportunity because of my previous experience as an international management consultant for the Alexander Proudfoot Company and my Asian studies background at Harvard and the University of Hawaii.) The project required me to tour throughout India and conduct economic development research that would assist Prime Minister Indira Gandhi in her efforts to improve her country. The project was timely, as she was also preparing for her first meeting with President Ronald Reagan (then in his first term).

President Reagan had just delivered his famous "Evil Empire" speech before the British House of Commons, where he called communist and socialist regimes "the axis of evil." While his words were clearly aimed at the Soviet Union, Mrs. Gandhi, the democratically elected head of the Socialist Party, was rightfully concerned as she was seeking the assistance of America to help modernize her country. Her administration was eager to modernize India and greatly desired American support and resources to do so.

My job was to study the effects indigenous village belief systems would have on villagers' willingness to accept the prime minister's modern changes. The major question was whether villagers with 99 percent illiteracy found modernizations like birth control, chemical additives to crops, and various new sanitation practices to be counter to their religious beliefs and practices. What if, for example, lifestyle changes like family planning were believed to create negative karmic consequences? What if something like the use of modern birth control was believed to adversely affect one's eternal soul? My objective was to find the answers.

These were significant considerations, not because the prime minister needed to outsmart her people but because successful, countrywide modernization required that her citizens be spiritually prepared for the changes she felt would ensure their best future. Prime Minister Gandhi understood that lasting behavioral change (no matter how well intended) would never take root and lead to significant improvement in the welfare of villagers (who make up most of the population of India) without first preparing these peoples' consciousness for change.

Like any great leader, Indira Gandhi intuitively understood the first of the Seven Arts for effective change: the Art of Preparation. It says that any leader of change must understand that the process first requires the mental and spiritual preparation of all parties affected. If the change itself, as well as the change process, is in sync with the collective mind of the people, then it will yield fruit. If it is not, the change process will fail every time.

WHERE ALL CHANGE BEGINS

Successful change can't happen because you have correctly manipulated your organization's culture. It can only happen when the desired change is aligned with the culture. In India, the prime minister understood that her modernization would be successful if it was in sync with the most widely held spiritual beliefs of the villagers, who were her culture's largest representation. I needed to determine what those spiritual beliefs were and then to specify how the modernization might best align with them.

In accord with what we experienced and learned about village life, the prime minister had instituted a unique form of government-supported rural education that would inform and prepare people for the health and economic changes ahead. She felt that once villagers understood how the changes would benefit them personally they would not resist them.

We now know she was right. Today, India is experiencing explosive modern growth. But the change would not have taken place had the ground not been made fertile nearly three decades ago through a strategy that ensured modernization would be understood and widely adopted. The lesson is in the basics.

If you want fresh coffee in the morning, you will have to take the additional preparatory step of grinding fresh beans. If you want a better body, you will have to get up earlier in the morning (or, perhaps more accurately, go to bed earlier the night before so that you aren't too tired to exercise). You might also have to store better food in your house so that when you're faced with food cravings, you are prepared to eat more healthily instead.

A friend once told me about the advice his grandfather—a Protestant minister—once gave him for getting the most value out of church. "Sunday morning," the grandfather asserted, "begins Saturday night." There is foundational truth in that statement. To achieve any change, one must prepare to achieve the result. Only in rare instances like unexpected tragedy or severe disaster do people actually change in a moment. Most changes are preceded by many moments of preparation.

But whether you invest in changing a nation or changing your coffee routine, the Art of Preparation is about laying a foundation that will ensure immediate and long-term success. Without the right foundation, the change process will not take hold and the effort will end in failure.

It should not be surprising that there is a 70 percent failure rate when companies try to change the culture or restructure. This is a failure rate that makes sense when one thinks about how difficult it is to sustain one positive change in your own life, like exercising more. The astronomical odds against leading a group of people to change their patterns of behavior simultaneously are clear.

Leaders of organizational change routinely underestimate the difficulty of change and do not dedicate the necessary resources in order to achieve the desired end. Most assume their people can be coerced to change. But trying to simply convince someone to change is no different than asking a smoker to quit just by telling him it's not good for him.*

A smoker doesn't smoke because he thinks it's good for him. He smokes because smoking feels better than not smoking. To lead a smoker to change, you must help him understand that there is greater pleasure on the other side of quitting. Until he is prepared at a deep level like this, he won't go through the pain of getting to the other side.

Clarifying the Drops

Imagine that the collective mind of your company is like a large bathtub of water. And imagine that the water is a brown muddy color that reflects the bad habits, negative thoughts, and counterproductive behaviors that must be changed for your company to survive. Let's also say that the desired business culture is represented by crystal-clear bath water.

Every time a person speaks or acts in your company, he or she puts a "drop" of water into the bathtub. Sometimes it's a brown muddy drop, and other times it is a crystal-clear drop. The culture of your company is always reinventing itself through the speech-drops and behavior-drops that enter the bath water.

---

* According to an article in the February 12, 2009, issue of *The New England Journal of Medicine* only 2 to 3 percent of smokers who try to quit each year are successful.

To lead positive change, you must ensure that everyone's drops are crystal clear because it is only after thousands of clear drops are put into the tub that the water begins to change.

Success requires that your people understand what words and actions represent clear drops and why these matter to them. This is why Prime Minister Gandhi took such great lengths to educate her people about the modernization she advocated before actually commencing the change. The education was an exercise in clarification at a spiritual level. This foundational exercise—what I call the Art of Preparation—is necessary in the corporate realm because it: (1) initiates the practice of spiritual development in your organization and (2) sets you up as the spiritual guide of lasting, meaningful change. The effect of this combination is unmatched by any other change strategy.

ORGANIZATIONAL CHANGE MUST EQUAL SPIRITUAL GROWTH

When you tie your company's desired change to the spiritual growth of your people, your employees have a compelling personal reason—the most compelling reason, in fact—not only to advocate the process but also to help propel it forward. This shared motive is a crucial ingredient for change.

There are five reasons this spiritual association serves as the best preparation for change:

> *1. People recognize that spiritual development is something of ultimate significance and importance.*

2. *People understand that a journey of spiritual development is both difficult and takes time.*

3. *People expect to take an honest and frank look at themselves with each step of a spiritual journey.*

4. *People know that spiritual development requires focus and therefore daily, even hourly, commitment.*

5. *People on a spiritual journey understand they must practice patience and discipline in order to resist the daily temptation to do things the way they have always been done.*

When your people equate organizational change with the process of deep personal growth, they attribute to it the same set of expectations as above. In sum, there is something unique, significant, and lasting in the effort for everyone. This makes all the difference.

Solidifying the Spiritual Association

With the importance of a spiritual basis for change now understood, we can turn to the key question: How does a leader make that happen? How can you ensure that your people equate organizational change with their own spiritual growth? To answer that question, we will simply turn the five statements about spirituality above into statements about your specific change effort. You'll notice we've just substituted *organizational change* in place of *spiritual development*:

1. People recognize that your organizational change is something of ultimate significance and importance.

Step back for a moment and consider your work life in relation to the rest of your life. People forget how much time we spend at work. Since you spend most of your waking hours at work, it makes sense to attach real meaning and significance to your commitments there.

Why should your people start their day thinking negatively about the place they spend most of their waking hours? Why should they only practice positive self-discipline during their limited time away from work? As part of the shared community that is your company, your people are presented daily with opportunities to develop interpersonal skills, leadership skills, and performance skills. Why shouldn't a time of genuine business crisis serve as an opportunity for everyone to actualize his or her best self? If you can reach people at that root level, you have the greatest chance of having them come on board your change mission.

Most leaders miss the fact that every employee possesses a latent willingness to change. Leaders often ignore the fact that personal progress is one of our strongest human desires. Your job as the leader is to connect the new business need with an opportunity for personal progress.

Because every organizational makeup is different—different numbers of people, different backgrounds, different interests and personal circumstances—I cannot tell you precisely how to do this. In the coming chapters, however, I will discuss further how your people can become more personally engaged in the change effort. Suffice it to say for now that each person must relate to the change at a personal level. The human resources (HR) manager must see that investing herself into the change effort will help her become a better mother, a better friend, a better person. The sales manager must see that investing himself into the effort will help him become a better father, friend, or husband.

When I consult, I often interview each person in the organization to determine how the change effort might serve every individual. I then provide the leader of the initiative with a snapshot of how the change lines up with his company's collective mind. This sort of knowledge is invaluable to preparing your people for change. (I have found that many leaders possess at least some personal knowledge of the individuals in their company to begin. What they do not know can often be filled in by managers and other supervisors who have a more day-to-day relationship with the people.)

Cultivating a personal association within every individual is important enough to make a concerted and genuine effort to ensure it. Some companies with whom I've worked spent up to three months on this first step. They came to see that when you sync organizational change with personal significance, the change process is met with little resistance.

2. People understand that the journey of organizational change is both difficult and takes time.

For years, I have sat through strategy sessions facilitated by other consultants serving my client in other function-specific capacities (for example, expanding markets and increasing sales). They often make things seem quite easy and, frankly, leave an organization with an unrealistic expectation of success. This is a bad place to begin because expectations establish the size of your fuel tank. If you think change will come quickly and easily, you'll run out of gas when nothing significant has occurred after six months. I see this a lot.

Once the function-specific professional consultants leave your office, I am the retained consultant asked to help you *execute* the new plan. After helping your company establish the first perception above, I then help you and your people see that execution in the real business world means approaching the change process with the same passion and commitment necessary for true spiritual development.

A phrase I often hear growth strategy consultants use is "seamless execution." The consultant points to the low end of a chart, and I know its coming; I can feel it. He says, "Right now you are here [tap, tap]. But with seamless execution your company will be enjoying this position [tapping the high end of the chart] in just two years." I am sitting in the meeting silently (for now) thinking that fortunately I know what these guys don't know. I know whether the collective mind of the company is yet ready for this seamless execution they speak of. I also know these well-meaning and highly intelligent consultants are missing an arrow in their quiver. Their thorough projections are without the most important consideration of all: the current spirit of the company. The truth is that my client is actually paying for some good experienced senior consultants, who make the presentation, as well as the student junior consultants, who actually collected the data and prepared the beautiful charts. Unfortunately, this group alone doesn't set the company up for successful change. At best, they whet their appetites for how things could be. It's not all bad, but it's not enough.

At this early stage of the change process, I am looking to fully prepare my client for success, which always includes telling the truth up front. People must know that the process will not be instantaneous or by any means simple—especially when it's company-wide. And the effort will be about a lot of other things before it's about seamless execution.

A recent client likened the change process to building a bonfire. "We placed the logs onto the pile first," he said. "And then once the bonfire pile (the infrastructure) for successful change had been built over three fiscal quarters, the change process publicly ignited." It is a realistic analogy.

Over the three-year change timeline, this same client experienced a 3,000 percent return on their investment as measured by their own productivity indicators. The change process was rolled out in the tumultuous textile industry whose labor was being largely outsourced overseas. The major personal incentive for my client's employees was to save their jobs. They understood up front that if they could dramatically improve performance, they would win the case for keeping labor in house—it was their best form of job security. It therefore wasn't difficult for them to comprehend the degree of difficulty in the change process. As the leader, it's your job to find that link between what matters most to your people and how the change effort will help them to achieve it. This will ensure a gritty, genuine effort to see the change through. Without this, your people are just doing their job. It's not enough to sustain most changes.

3. **People expect to take an honest and frank look at themselves with each step of the organizational change, which includes actively seeking feedback to expose their hidden weaknesses and subconscious devices.**

Being prepared for change requires collective self-assessment, which includes a willingness to receive and act on negative feedback. Effective spiritual development requires understanding weaknesses, devices, and attachments that cause an individual to be less than his best self. Similarly, your organization must proactively seek feedback and create an environment that encourages and facilitates open communication to uncover any hidden hurdles to the change process.

I like to call this an environment of *bulletproof* communication because no one shoots the messenger and everyone actively seeks bad news because they are protected. A client's plant manager once declared his factory's change mantra was, "Bad news is good news if it is given early." It's not a bad way to think.

Companies without this kind of thinking are easy to spot; it takes about five minutes. You can actually feel the politics slithering through the office—the posturing, the gamesmanship. And these companies always struggle to change even the smallest procedure because the unspoken rules say no one can handle the truth.

Let's put it this way: Your company's change efforts will rarely fail because of your strengths. It is your weaknesses, your hidden hurdles, which will hold you back or take you down. Uncovering weaknesses up front makes it possible to eliminate their threat to the change process. In this case, defense is a great offense.

I always set out to learn as much about a client as possible. I look at the financials, board presentations, and company strategy. I attend senior management meetings and other meetings throughout the company to observe the collective mind of the business. I conduct confidential, one-on-one interviews with approximately 200 people from all functions and all levels of leadership. I learn enough to give honest feedback to the chief executive officer (CEO), and if he or she can't take it, I know there's a serious problem. If I assess a company and the communication is not open and honest, and it seems like the CEO does not want critical feedback, there are only two options: (1) I walk out the door telling them their company is hurting due to a cancerous environment, or (2) I test the waters, push back hard, and explain why and how an open and honest environment is needed. This is always a defining moment.

In fact, for this reason it is now common practice that I insist on the following:

- The CEO personally hires me (not the human resources senior executive)
- I report directly to the CEO
- He or she gives me complete access to his or her schedule
- He or she understands why time for change management activities will be required in significant quantities
- That honesty and bulletproof communication become the norm between us and everybody else

These criteria are not a lot to ask if the company is engaged in the most difficult challenge it has ever faced, or at least one that must happen for it to survive.

The Art of Preparation requires your company to lay out the realities of the present state of the business. Identifying the real interpersonal challenges you face at the outset gives you the ideal opportunity to create change plans that avoid the collaboration and communication mistakes of the past.

Resistance to change is normal, even when the perception about it is positive and necessary. Resistance to positive change often happens subconsciously when blind spots and egos stand in the way of clearly assessing your current standing. Without accurate assessment, your company is vulnerable to being blind-sided. It is absolutely necessary to get the truth on the table.

4. People know that organizational change requires focus and therefore daily, even hourly, commitment.

Anyone involved in a change of thinking or behavior must learn to practice new habits on a daily basis. Habits are not easily changed, and so daily focus is tantamount. The same is true of organizational change. Daily, "drop-by-drop" behavior is the only level of focus that will produce measurable, sustainable changes in everyone's performance. It is the only way the water will clear up. When such results occur—when change becomes tangible—the new habits get a strong dose of momentum and positive reinforcement. This first taste of positive change strengthens the collective belief that the new ways of performing and conducting business are indeed better for all involved.

It is critical to communicate visible evidence that reinforces changes in the invisible collective mind. In fact, the use of visible metrics makes leading change easier in the business arena than in personal development because they put everyone on the same page and initiate accountability throughout the company. In this case, the herd mentality works in your favor as collective expectations climb and people begin holding their own actions and those of others to the new standard. All want to succeed, and where leading change is concerned, there is no greater fuel for success than success. (A more thorough explanation of the use of visible evidence or metrics appears in Chapter 4 as part of the

Art of Relaxation. Such metrics help employees "relax" because they know what counts, they learn how to focus, and they eliminate all energy being directed to off-strategy activities.)

5. People in an organizational change process understand they must practice patience and discipline in order to resist the daily temptation to do things the way they have always done them.

In publicly traded companies where quarterly reporting is the norm, there is incredible pressure on the entire organization to achieve performance targets previously established and monitored under the watchful eye of Wall Street and industry analysts. Often this pressure is manifested within the organization in the form of short-term firefighting near the conclusion of every quarter. This causes the organization to lose focus on the long-term change process.

When productivity or quality problems develop that affect the cost side of the financial equation, or when there are downwardly revised revenue forecasts, people inside the company often retreat into their old, habituated way of doing things. This can kill a change effort.

It takes great courage and consistency to help people stick with new ways of thinking and behaving when the quarterly pressure cooker is boiling. It is natural for people to retreat when this happens. Therefore, practicing the Art of Preparation must include setting realistic expectations for the imminent collisions between performance targets and the change effort. If you do not prepare for these challenges at the outset, sustaining your change amidst outside pressure from the public eye, a board, or otherwise will feel like changing the tires on a car while it is moving at 70 miles per hour.

THE ART OF PREPARATION

Leading change is an art not a science in the sense that you cannot lay out a six- or eight- or ten-step cookie cutter process for success. Effectively preparing your organization for change is little more than an artist gathering his unique combination of paints and brushes and then discovering the location that will inspire the masterpiece. Your people are your unique paints and brushes, and the location of your change masterpiece is a culture that associates the change with spiritual growth and personal significance. This occurs when the five perceptions we've just discussed are adopted by your people. Here they are again, in brief:

First, the rationale for and the benefits of the change effort must be spiritually anchored in every individual involved. Each one must perceive the corporate change initiative as equivalent to a personal growth initiative like losing weight or quitting smoking.

Second, the people must accurately perceive the difficulty and time-length of the process.

Third, the people must perceive that a new level of open and honest, bulletproof communication will be required in order to avoid the mistakes and false starts of the past.

Fourth, the people must perceive that successful change will require a daily commitment to new behavior, individually and corporately.

Fifth, the people must perceive that change not only upsets the status quo—the way things have always been done—but also causes new and unforeseen problems that they must be prepared to address and overcome.

Buying into all five perceptions is a lot for even an executive team to swallow, let alone the whole organization. But my experience is that the change initiative will fail without the entire organization on board and in sync in this way. My experience is also that change leaders ultimately want realistic expectations, no-nonsense talk, and a strategy with a track record of successful, profitable change in a variety of industries. I tell them what I will tell you; this is such a strategy. It's not going to happen overnight, but if you follow it, you will be successful.

I understand that investing in change can be a scary proposition. Change is at first an intangible sale, not unlike buying advertising. When you agree to buy from the ad agency, you do not know whether the commercial, for example, will translate into sales. My experience is that companies get taken for a ride when they invest in a strategy that is not first established at a deep, spiritual level in their people. That is why the Art of Preparation is so critical. Without it, you remain on a sandy foundation that can easily be moved by the ebbing and flowing tide. And in business, the tide ebbs and flows incessantly.

Your organization must establish a firm foundation of mutual trust and respect during the Art of Preparation. It requires something outside the comfort zone for everyone, including the leader. But for you to become the established, accepted spiritual guide for your company—and lead them to successful change—you must embody this first Art wholeheartedly.

How will this organizational change grow you personally? You must also know this and be willing to embrace it as a real personal benefit of the process. Are you willing to confront your character shortcomings or past failures in leading the company? You must listen and learn for the sake of yourself and the process. You will fail to lead successful change if you are not willing to allow yourself to change. Are you realistic about the difficulty and length of the process? Your people will not stay the course if you allow them to believe it will be quick and painless. And they will not stay committed when the going gets tough if they are not prepared for the temptation to fall back on old habits.

These are the initial realities of any successful, worthwhile change: it is personally challenging and beneficial; it requires personal sacrifice, humility, and commitment; and it requires a solid, deep-rooted foundation that inspires all activity. When you create these realities in your spirit and the spirit of your people, your organization is prepared for positive, profitable change.

· 2 ·

THE ART OF COMPASSION

CONFLICT IS THE NATURE OF CHANGE. This is true in the individual experience as well as the corporate experience. To lose weight, for instance, your old eating habits come into conflict with the new habits you must form. The change process always contains a rub that is best described as one energy (the old agenda) in conflict against another energy (the new initiative). Both individuals and companies get themselves into trouble when they assume they can force change to occur.

The problem is that pushing through new habits uses up a tremendous amount of energy—energy that will be critical for sustaining the momentum of the change once it has begun to stick. It is far too common for a company to implement a change initiative and even begin to see it's initial rewards and then, seemingly out of nowhere, start falling off pace and reverting to old patterns. Such companies are like the boxer who comes out swinging in the first two rounds and then finds himself flat on his back in the third round because he punched himself out and was then caught with his hands down. He overused his energy trying to force himself on his opponent. But instead of gaining the victory, his forceful effort worked against him.

To successfully lead change in any organization, you must understand the spiritual essence of what is happening: the energy required to implement your new habits (the positive, "progressive" energy) is coming into conflict with the energy required to maintain the status quo (the negative, "resistant" energy). Ultimately the energy that wins is the one that utilizes the conflicting energy to compound itself, not the one that forces the other into submission. This is the essence of the Art of Compassion.

When I explain this spiritual dynamic of change to large audiences, I often do so through a demonstration of the martial art of *Ki-Aikido*, known as a "compassionate" martial art. The idea behind *Ki-Aikido* is to defend yourself, disarm your opponent if necessary, and then immobilize him without using excessive force. During a conflict, you simply utilize the negative energy your opponent gives you—a strike, a punch, a kick—to neutralize his attack peacefully. Instead of returning a fierce right hand, you move aside (quickly, of course) and allow the force of that punch to compound your effort to lead/throw your opponent to the ground in the same direction and then quickly immobilize him. It does not take much energy to "throw" a man—even a very large one—when he has given you the opportunity to "lead" with the full force of his energy.

This dynamic is just as effective in organizational settings where resistance to change can be an intensely strong force. When your company learns to channel this negative energy into the positive energy of compassion, your company actually compounds energy through the change process instead of losing it. This allows you and your people to sustain momentum throughout the effort, instead of punching yourselves out, dropping your hands, and taking one on the chin.

This does not mean the change process suddenly becomes easy. On the contrary, the process still requires a well-prepared, concerted effort. But instead of expending all your energy forcing out the old habits, your people learn to transform the negative, resistant energy they all feel into unique, daily opportunities to strengthen the momentum of change.

I'll explain this further with a story of how the Art of Compassion came to be an integral part of my corporate change regimen.

TURNING CONFLICT INTO COMPASSION

The famous writer Hunter Thompson, author of *Fear and Loathing in Las Vegas*, lived in Aspen and decided in 1970 that he would run for sheriff on an ultra-leftist platform. In addition to his rather unusual and unconventional ideas about law enforcement, Thompson wanted to work with the Aspen City Council in order to replace the streets in downtown Aspen with grass. In his way of thinking, this would ensure the absence of automobile pollution as well as the protection of local pedestrians who might be struck by cars traveling on the icy asphalt.

Thompson lost the 1970 election but his understudy, a man named Richard "Dick" Kienast, was elected six years later when the sheriff that defeated Thompson was forced to resign midterm. It was shortly after this time that Dick read Sissela Bok's new book *Lying: Moral Choice in Public and Private Life*. From this inspired work, Dick found his philosophical focus as well as his public voice, citing Shakespeare's *Othello* in his acceptance speech for it's portrayal of the tragedy of persons, family, and state that can occur when there exists a complete breakdown of trust. Dick asked himself the question I would ask you as a leader of change: "Have you ever wondered if you could take your best ideas and put them into practice?"

Dick responded to the challenge of using his political office to better society. His campaign poster cited Bok's work—a testament to how society might be: "Trust is a social good to be protected just as much as the air we breathe or the water we drink." Dick believed that trustworthy compassion, not force, was a better and more effective strategy whether dealing with a violent felon or simply a frustrated traffic offender. And he believed this spirit of law enforcement was necessary in order to earn the trust of the Pitkin County residents. It was a momentous change initiative and one that many thought foolish and unnecessary (perhaps not unlike a change that your company needs to undertake). Nevertheless, he moved forward in confidence.

About this time my long-time friend Tom Crum asked me to teach *Ki-Aikido* at the Aspen-Snowmass Academy of Martial Arts just up the road from downtown Aspen. Among my first students were Sheriff Dick Kienast and his deputies. (I would later become one of Dick's deputy sheriffs myself.) These men and women would go on to establish a legacy of the Art of Compassion in Pitkin County that still reverberates today. One of

Kienast's deputies, Bob Braudis, once had an experience that epitomizes the power of this second Art.

Bob was one of those first deputies I met. He later succeeded Dick Kienast as sheriff of Pitkin County where he remains today. Bob's large, imposing physical presence fit people's stereotype of the hard-nosed, no-nonsense cop. But despite his appearance, he was one of the best examples of turning conflict into compassion I've ever encountered. Bob never raised his voice or expressed anger with arrestees, even in potentially violent situations. Whether it was a domestic fight, a kidnapping, a felony arrest, or a simple civil disturbance, his nonviolent approach always lead everyone to a calm, productive place. In a hostage situation, for example, we're used to seeing police cars with lights blazing and officers with bullhorns trying to communicate with gun-toting, deranged kidnappers, creating a volatile situation. However, with Bob's calm, steady presence, I saw that everything could change—particularly the outcome—when the negative energy of conflict was turned into a powerful tool for positive change.

One event is case in point. Bob was patrol director, and a call came through dispatch that a gunman was holding all the patrons at Woody Creek Tavern hostage. Bob was the first to arrive on the scene. From outside the restaurant, he calmly assessed the situation and then approached the window. Rather than being confrontational, Bob sought to understand the gunman's issues and state of mind. The man had separated from his wife, and she would not let him see his daughter. Now, he had seen his little girl in the restaurant and decided to hold her and the rest of the patrons hostage.

Reasoning with the man would seem fruitless to most, but Bob understood the power behind the Art of Compassion. He knew that he could disarm the man if he used the man's negative energy to compound the positive energy he was bringing to the conflict. In this case, Bob did so through a strategy of listening and understanding. He sensed that beneath the man's outer rage was an inner pain grounded in a deep love for his daughter. He was just manifesting his pain in a potentially harmful—even lethal—way. And it was not really directed at his daughter or the patrons of Woody Creek Tavern.

Sensing Bob's compassion, the gunman allowed Bob to enter the building unarmed. Bob then proceeded to speak calmly to the man. He led him to pause and consider his actions that would put him behind bars for a long time at best, and forever if he killed someone. As a result of these actions, Bob explained, he might not ever see his daughter again. Did he really want to run that risk?

Bob's placid demeanor, his rational discussion of the real issues, and his empathy toward the man's rage validated the suspect. All the man really wanted was for people to know that someone had done him wrong and his pain was almost unbearable. In short, Bob put himself in the man's shoes, and the more the man talked with Bob, the more he realized that much of his anger was with himself. He eventually put down his weapon.

The man's whole demeanor then changed. And true to his Art, Bob suggested ways to get the gunman safely out of the situation. He asked him to kindly put on handcuffs for his own safety. Bob explained that exiting the tavern with cuffs on would put all the law enforcement people outside the tavern at ease so that neither Bob nor the suspect would run the risk of being shot. The man complied, and the conflict was ended peacefully.

CHANGING THROUGH COMPASSION

There was nothing particularly complicated about what Bob Braudis did. He was merely transforming the *Ki* (energy) of the entire situation. He instinctively knew that a policeman's aggressive, power-charged actions would not intimidate the hostage-taker into submission; they would actually heighten his resistance. And if neither side backed down, it would build to an uncontrollable tension that might not end well.

Bob saw, as did his mentor Dick, that a compassionate approach was more powerful and ultimately more successful in handling conflict. The same is true in an organizational setting. Practicing the Art of Compassion in the corporate world means transforming the negative energy of change initiatives with the subtle force of a calm, compassionate connection. When your people are stressed, angry, or hypersensitive to anything outside the way things have always been done, you can effectively neutralize their negative energy with a calm, spiritual approach to the change process. This sets the stage. It is the equivalent of Bob approaching the window peacefully and entering the building unarmed.

Once the initial negative energy of change is neutralized, you can convert it into positive energy. To do so, you must help your people see the natural conflicts that arise when change is being implemented as opportunities to display compassion to one another. In this way the energy required for change ramps up instead of down, and the initiative can be sustained with increasingly less effort.

The Leader's Role

When I walk into a consulting situation, I am like that hostage-taker, only with a different motive. I have an agenda that most of those in the building don't know about. I am an outsider, and I pose a threat to the status quo. People are immediately defensive. If I react to their defensiveness in any way they construe as aggressive or retaliatory, they will escalate their response by becoming more defensive. This will only make my job more difficult. Knocking them back on their heels will make them far less willing to be a participant in the endeavor we are undertaking, and it will establish or reinforce a leadership-versus-employees mentality.

Few people like to be criticized or judged. Overcoming the perception that I am judge and jury and getting people to drop their "who do you think you are?" stance is one of the first things I have to do in working with individual or organizational clients. This is where compassion initially comes into play for any leader of change. If we are going to co-create a culture in which participation is at the highest and most inspired level, compassion must inspire all activity.

One thing I have learned in nearly three decades of consulting is that organizations are living things and are therefore subject to the same principles as the individuals who make up that organization. There are some basic, underlying concepts to this truth that I'd like to help you understand because they will give you and your people a spiritual foundation for applying the Art of Compassion to your organization's change initiative right away, before the negative energy takes over.

Relative Thinking vs. Absolute Thinking

When you see and experience your organization as a single entity of which you are a part, then you break through the confines of what philosophers call *relative thinking*. Relative thinking is a negative notion that we exist separate and apart from the remainder of the universe—in other words, we live disconnected from the people and energies that make up our reality.

When you are boarding a bus and an elderly person ahead of you is taking a great deal of time to find a token, you get angry because you are going to be late for an appointment. You have engaged in relative thinking because you are subscribing to the notion that only your agenda, actions, and outcomes are what matters in the world.

When you take a "that's good enough" attitude into your work endeavors and don't consider how your lackadaisical efforts will impact others in the organization, you are also thinking relatively. My experience is that most organizations consist of people who think in this manner. But this is often the case because no one has ever explained to them the spiritual basis for another kind of thinking.

Relative thinking is contrasted by *absolute thinking*: the philosophy that we all exist together in interconnected fashion. Compassion is an outgrowth of absolute thinking because it is the highest way to ensure your actions toward others impact the whole in positive fashion—the whole of which you are an integral part.

Absolute thinking engenders the strongest kind of participation that always aims for what is best for everyone—for the entire organization. This is not merely good teamwork we are talking about. Absolute thinking is a spiritual paradigm that inspires compassionate participation because all involved understand and believe—as Sheriff Bob Braudis did—that it is the most effective path to progress.

To begin to awaken yourself and your people to the reality of living in a compassionate, interconnected universe—in particular, your "organizational universe"—consider how your mere entrance into a room changes everything.

You might enter a meeting in progress, or a bedroom at home where your spouse is on the phone, or walk in on your children engaged in watching cartoons. You do not need to say anything. Your mere presence observed by the others changes their consciousness, their words, even their actions.

Your colleagues invite you to join the meeting . . . your spouse looks up and smiles . . . your children ask you to help them find a particular crayon. This is more than the result of mere interruption. Energy is constantly being exchanged in this dynamic, ever-changing universe. When you walk into the room, the energy in the room changes, for better or worse. The examples above are positive ones, but as we all know, this isn't always the case.

I often illustrate this point with my philosophy students. I walk into the classroom with an armload of graded term papers as the unsuspecting students wait with anticipation (or anxiety). I walk slow, head down, and say nothing. I pause at the front of the room behind my lectern. I then look into their curious eyes and drop the entire stack of papers onto the table beside me. Crash! I glare at them and assert, "I have graded all your term papers and made very, very extensive comments." All the social chatter is transformed into dead silence. They are terrified.

I let this silence become uncomfortable for a moment. Then I smile and say, "Fortunately this brief classroom exercise has been an act. You can all relax now. I am not returning your term papers today."

The energy of the room immediately changes again, and I explain that the day's lecture is about the interconnectedness of all things.

"The energy of the universe is not just physical energy," I tell them. "I believe that all of you just experienced this phenomenon. You could all feel the energy of the entire classroom change. Moreover, you experienced your personal energy change during today's exercise. Energy is constantly being exchanged. The fact is inescapable."

Because of this constant exchange, compassion and interconnectedness are critical in all areas of life. And when it comes to organizational success—especially success with change initiatives—I do not know of a company who has sustained necessary, positive change without understanding the implication of these activities at a spiritual level and then applying them company-wide. This must be an early, established goal of all leaders of change. You must introduce the initiative (a.k.a., enter the room) with absolute thinking and a keen understanding of what is about to happen to the energy of your people.

Introducing the Art of Compassion

The first step to enacting the Art of Compassion is always awareness. This must be modeled by the leader without exception. I am keenly aware in any consulting situation of the power and effect of my presence. I know that merely being present in the building immediately alters the dynamic—most often negatively. I have to do as much as I can from the very beginning to make certain that I mitigate my influence by establishing myself, first, as a neutral presence and then later as a positive presence. This is typically also the case when the leader of change stands up and delivers the "change is on the horizon" speech, memo, or e-mail. People immediately worry about job security, salary reductions, and a host of other altered conditions they perceive will negatively affect their lives.

This is all to say that at the outset of initiatives, the perception of forthcoming change nearly always creates a force of negative energy not unlike that of the hostage-taker in Woody Creek Tavern. This is the conflict rearing its head. As the leader, you must be keenly aware of it and then know how to transform it into positive momentum through compassion.

Unfortunately, compassion does not naturally occur to people—leaders or otherwise—in such situations because we get wrapped up in ourselves. We get selfish and preoccupied with the individual consequences. In short, we slip into relative thinking—"I'm alone in this . . . How will it affect me?"—when we should be engaged in absolute thinking—"We're in this together . . . How can we make it work?"

It is so easy to feel isolated when we are members of a large organization. Unfortunately, the hierarchical structures designed to help organizations function smoothly wind up creating obstacles to interconnectedness. But these obstacles are largely created by us; they are not, as we'd like to think, merely fundamental, necessary evils.

For some reason, we've conditioned ourselves to believe that business, capitalism, and management are subjects for which the laws of compassion and interconnectedness do not apply. For some reason, under the façade of "it's nothing personal; it's just business," we excuse behavior we would normally consider insensitive, careless, cruel, and even abusive. As a result, we fire up the change engines and scream down the new path with a strategy that burns energy, burns trust, and burns momentum.

Burnout, dissatisfaction, and a never-ending cycle of fits and starts all remain realities because the only things uniting us are the four walls we share. In this setting, benefits and incentives don't serve their purpose because people still see a greater benefit in avoiding the pain of change than pursuing the pleasure on the other side of change.

Why this unemotional, spiritually deficient approach still has advocates is beyond me. Connectedness and compassion are the centerpieces of true change leadership, and without them your organization will continually butt against the negative energy arising from new initiatives. Unless you lead your people to use the conflict of change in a positive way, the effort will lose momentum. This begins when you acknowledge the negative energy present and then begin to model the compassion that will turn the negative energy around. Every one of us has experienced the impact of this sort of leadership in our lives.

Think about one of the most effective leaders you've ever had. Whether a leader by position, such as a teacher, a boss, a parent, or a coach, or an informal leader, such as a teammate, a co-worker, or a close friend—what drew you to this person? What feeling did you have when you were around this person that was so strong you still remember it today? What particular memory sticks in your mind about your relationship with this person?

Odds are high that the memory flashing through your mind is one in which the person did little more than listen to you as you dealt with an important situation. Your "life coach" might not have even offered advice. The influence came from a strong ability to understand you, empathize with you, and then help you do your best. The bond between you likely became so strong that you would do just about anything for them—even today.

We all willingly follow and model a leader who makes an effort to truly understand us. That is because such leaders exude compassion. Recall the emotions you initially felt during that situation in which your leader helped you. I'm sure fear and apprehension were a significant portion of your emotional energy. Recall how that leader's presence and actions guided you toward a positive resolution and personal growth and how those actions transformed your energy.

In the same way, leaders in an organization must show compassion for the fear and apprehension employees feel as they face the uncertainty of change at work. People under stress often act contrary to their usual nature.

While teaching *Ki-Aikido* to Sheriff Kienast and his deputies, I was asked to become a deputy myself as the training budget could not afford for me to only teach martial arts. I joined my students as a sworn deputy, and during my ensuing law enforcement career in Aspen, I saw many examples of basically good people doing bad things because they were under a great deal of stress or emotional angst. When suspects of violent crime are emotionally sick, disabled, or torn apart over a loved one, for example, it's a critical time to remember our shared humanity. Experiences like this were invaluable lessons for me to learn before my change management career had begun. I came to see that lasting change could not occur without an element of compassion.

THE KEY: COMPASSION LEADS TO TRUST; TRUST LEADS TO PARTICIPATION

While the hostage-taker is an extreme example, a fundamental pillar of the Art of Compassion is understanding that the people in your organization are probably all good people who can quickly grow stressed and despondent about changes that might severely affect their entire lives. In such situations, people will often act out, exposing their greatest fears and anxieties in ugly ways. By approaching them as Sheriff Braudis did the hostile father, in a way that is understanding of their fears, it is possible to neutralize the negative energy they put forth in the initial stages of change. Instead of throwing gasoline on the conflict, you lead the spirit of the conflict—and thus the spirit of the company—to a neutral place where reason and positive emotion can be introduced.

Bar none, the most effective and practical way to accomplish this is through the act of listening. I don't know of another more compassionate activity than listening and then responding in a way that demonstrates genuine understanding. There is so much power in this small act because it can immediately establish trust and diffuse the negative energy exuding from individuals at the outset of change. No speech, act, or intervention can accomplish such a deep measure of trust in such a short time. And trust is what you are after.

My first measurable goal in helping an organization through the change process is to generate genuine employee participation. This is the ultimate outgrowth of the Art of Compassion, and the bridge between compassion and participation is trust.

Encompassing the change effort with compassion establishes trust—trust in the leadership and trust in the change—even when nothing has yet happened. Your people begin to trust that you care about what they are going through and will go through. That you care it will not be a simple, stress-free process for them. When your people begin to trust their leaders, they can then trust the change that leadership is asking of them. When they trust the change, they can participate with full ownership rather than "I'll do it because I'm supposed to" obligation.

Consider the vast difference between the Woody Creek father's actions when (1) he first took the tavern hostage and (2) when he handed the sheriff his gun and slipped on his own handcuffs. In scenario one, his actions were hostile and violent. Even if he never laid a hand on a single person, his actions were a strong force of negative energy. A furious right-hand punch. Then, in less than thirty minutes, he was willingly surrendering his gun, his hands . . . and ultimately his spirit to Bob's force of positive energy. The sum of what happened is this: the deputy's compassion compelled the father's trust, and the father then fully participated in the "change" of circumstances Bob led him through.

Your organization must deploy this same spiritual level of participation in order to sustain its change. Everyone must be willing to stretch, adjust, and challenge themselves to do their part. They must participate from the spirit inside them that compels action from a foundation of trust, reciprocity, and desire for personal growth.

Compassionate listening and understanding establishes this standard of participation. It compels people to care about the change rather than complain about it or confront it. My lifelong *Ki-Aikido* teacher and mentor, Master Tohei, calls this "putting yourself in the place of your partner." It is one of the tenets of success in the martial art of *Ki-Aikido*, and it is just as important in your organizational change efforts.

Taking Inventory before You Begin

It is important to know where you and your people stand before initiating the Art of Compassion. I have often found that leaders have done a lot of damage to their people in the trust department. They've shown little to no compassion over a period of time and as a result their people couldn't care less about what the leader was about to ask them to do. This, unfortunately, is more common than I care to admit. But one thing is certain. The level of anger, pain, and even hostility such people are feeling is not unlike that of the anguished father. Their negative energy can be transformed just as his was.

The trick is that you can't fake compassion. If that father had sensed for a second that Sheriff Braudis' actions were a cover, there is no telling how ugly the scene would have gotten. To feel and convey compassion, you must truly put yourself in another's shoes and take on a portion of what he or she might feel right then. I've found this is easier for leaders to comprehend when I remind them that they weren't always CEOs, executive vice presidents (EVPs), or chief operating officers (COOs). And the truth is that no leader of change enters the process without his or her own portion of anxiety and fear. It would be a banner day were a leader to actually admit to employees that significant change is never without personal doubt and uncertainty. What a start that would be.

There are telling behaviors like this, which indicate the current level of compassion in you and your organization. It is important to know which of the following behaviors you and your people embody and which you do not before enacting the Art of Compassion full force. When reading through the following list, consider where you stand with these certain behaviors as well as where the collective behavior of your organization stands:

Behaviors: Authenticity and Accessibility

- Employees are in the moment. Communication isn't done on the run and with half attention.

- Employees are purposeful. Present conversations and collaborations (in person, on phone, or via e-mail) get to the essence of the issue.

- Employees are accessible. Access is easy at least two levels above.

- Employees trust their managers and the organization's direction.
- Disagreement is acceptable.
- Belittlement is unacceptable.

Behaviors: Abundance and Unity

- Employees can describe the bigger picture and their role in it.
- Employees offer unfiltered feedback without fear of repercussions.
- Leaders accept the truth without punishing the messenger.
- Information, ideas, and experience are shared.
- Contribution has a high value no matter who it comes from.
- There appear to be no "favorites."
- Managers view one of the key purposes of their job to be helping their staff develop personally and professionally, even if it means members will be promoted and move on.
- The benefits of improvements are shared with employees.

Behavior: Clear, Open Communication

- Employees know what is going on in the industry and in the company.
- Employees understand the thought process and metrics behind decisions, especially those that impact them directly.
- Objectives are clear and consistent with rewards.
- Silos are minimal at worst and nonexistent at best.
- Policies exist that evidence trust in the basic worth and work ethic of each individual.
- When mistakes are made, the focus is on a solution rather than affixing blame and punishment.

I recommend this inventory because I know that compassion must become and remain part of the culture in order to give the change initiative a chance. Using compassion to get people to accept change but then returning to the old ways of doing things will destroy whatever trust was established. It is the equivalent of Bob Braudis getting in the door of the tavern with a display of compassion and then trying to wrestle the father to the ground with brute force. His odds of success don't necessarily improve if the man merely lets him in the door, and yours won't either. Compassion must spread and continue if your people are to stay fully engaged. It is not a pick up now-and-then sort of tool. It must be a mainstay in the hands of everyone.

The key is ensuring that the behaviors are not only (1) practiced on a regular basis but also (2) modeled by yourself and the other leaders, and then (3) reinforced through predetermined check-ins and performance-based benefits. When I worked with Duracell, it was particularly important to establish a daily practice of compassionate behaviors in everyone because this was a large, multinational company. For the negative energy of change to be diffused and widespread participation to occur, the Art of Compassion needed to spread quickly and thickly. This meant holding large group meetings where each of the goals and initiatives of the change were explained. We placed a particular emphasis on each individual's role in making those goals achievable. More importantly, leadership had to take the extra step of explaining how the intended result was connected uniquely to each individual depending upon which piece of the larger puzzle was his or hers.

In order to be a world-class producer of batteries, all employees must perceive themselves to be world-class. For example, regardless of how large the Duracell conglomerate was, it still had to have world-class players at every position, including the receptionists at every location. In fact, talking about the important interconnected role of the Duracell receptionists was the favorite example of Duracell CEO Bob Kidder. Such employees were not only responsible for every outsider's first impression of the conglomerate, they were also the first to bear the burden of dealing with less-than-cordial interactions and ensuring VIPs were appropriately supported. Managers had to go deeper to understand what it was receptionists, for instance, really did on an everyday basis, what kinds of issues they encountered (emotional, physical, psychological, etc.), and then fine-tune their understanding of that role as it pertained to their responsibilities.

To accomplish this with every employee took more than feigned compassion (i.e., "I understand your job can be tough, but I still need more from you"). It took stepping deeper into the spirit of each receptionist in the organization and aligning the initiative according to the understanding that was received there via listening. By not pushing back against the anxieties, stresses, and unknown obstacles each receptionist felt, the change agents (the department managers, in this case) thus laid the trustworthy groundwork for compassion. They got in the door. Once there, they could then transform the receptionists' personal conflict of change into positive participation by establishing guidelines for performance that took into account the difficulty of the receptionists'/all employees' primary challenges.

After the initial group meetings and the subsequent individual follow-up interviews, there was an enormous and instantaneous difference in the performance of the receptionists/all employees. In short, every "player of the field" eventually came to see that (1) they mattered as individual employees and (2) their work mattered in the change process. They were thus quickly and deeply motivated to participate in a far more thorough manner. This evaluation, connection, and compassion process was successfully introduced throughout every subset of the entire Duracell organization.

While applying the same strategy was always a little different with each company with whom I worked, and depended largely on the current collective mind, the following characteristics have been the most common evidences that the Art of Compassion is spreading throughout an organization. These benchmarks evidence specific characteristics that can be used to establish guidelines for everyday activity as well as standards for measuring performance once your initiative has begun.

Signs of a Compassion-Oriented Organization That Encourages Full Employee Participation

1. *Performance-based compensation is welcomed.* If you want people to think and act like an owner, then make them a real owner. People care and participate like owners when they can actively create wealth for all stakeholders—themselves included. Ownership in the company is thus a reality that is motivated and therefore sustained through a compassionate understanding of everyone's obstacles to success and current challenges to greater performance.

2. *Listening is institutionalized.* Organizations that evidence compassion listen to each other in order to understand and connect to more effective outcomes, not in order to place blame or assert their own way of doing things. Listening is the root of collaboration, root-cause analysis, and effective teamwork. It is also

the single greatest source of establishing unity from top to bottom and bottom to top.

3. *People trust each other. Trust is earned.* Compassion-oriented organizations have a track record of treating people respectfully no matter their position or seniority. Belittling or judging people only raises the tension of conflicts because it polarizes people and promotes solving problems through head-to-head battle (which saps energy) rather than the reallocation of energy (which increases energy).

4. *People grow and develop together.* Organizations can be a vehicle for powerful personal development. They invest in and create conditions for people to succeed holistically and be the best they can be on and off the job. This shows a high measure of compassion to all employees the conditions effect.

5. *Boardroom awareness is an ongoing reality.* In many ways, we all remain kids at heart. Even as adults, we still want to know why we are being asked to do something. "Because I told you so" in the corporate setting does nothing more for adults than it did for them as children. It usually creates more questions, more conflict, and power struggles that squash the opportunity for understanding and education. Compassion-focused businesses are education-focused organizations. They build in regular opportunities to help every employee

understand some things: why we are changing now . . . which competitors wish to drive us out of business . . . and how our financial performance is related to each person's job. If every employee understands the business like a board member, then the competitive urgency for change is well understood by everyone without the enormous adverse effects created by an angry manager who threatens with a verbal whip.

6. *People connect with each other.* When people are understood and are offered understanding of the business, they care. When this situation exists, you can rid yourself of an entire layer of management whose sole purpose seems to be to police people so the inmates do not cause a riot.

7. *Authority matches responsibility.* If you have an integrity-based culture where people regularly do what they say, you can rid yourself of more needless decision-making hierarchy that slows the organization down. Compassion-based organizations pass the authority down so that everyone can make on-the-spot decisions wherever and whenever they are needed in order to get the job done.

8. *The Golden Rule is modeled and embraced.* Compassion-oriented organizations make a habit of everyone putting themselves in the place of their co-worker. Problems are solved quickly and painlessly

(without wasting energy) when everyone develops the habit of facing individual problems as one.

9. *Communication is honest.* Compassion-based businesses foster honesty across the board. Politics, grandstanding, and backstabbing are not tolerated. The most compassionate organization protects itself from the double standard where the privileged few are allowed to not walk the talk. Acting in accord with organizational values is key, lest everyone become cynical. The compassionate culture is a human culture where words and character matter.

The Force of Compassion

I will admit that I always have doubters when it comes to the power of compassion to overcome conflict. I will often, in the right setting of course, offer a tangible demonstration of this power to make the point clear and memorable. One of the largest doubters, literally, was a Pitkin County, Colorado, undersheriff named Don Davis, a 6-foot-5-inch, 260-pound force of muscle. Sheriff Dick Kienast and his band of merry men and women— of which I was now an official part as a deputy and in-house *Ki-Aikido* trainer—were called the "peacemakers," and we all knew that someone needed to show us how to become real police officers. Dick was affectionately known as "The Dove," and he attracted like-minded people eager to make a difference but who were generally inexperienced in law enforcement. The career police officer we all looked up to (and feared) was Don Davis.

Hailing from Las Cruces, New Mexico, Big Don wore snug Levis and tight turtlenecks that highlighted the muscular bulges covering his body. Before Don, only my father got away with calling me anything but "David." Don called me "Davey." I came to see it was a sign of affection that occurred immediately after our initial encounter where we really got to know each other.

Passing the Test

On the first day of our *Ki-Aikido* arrest control class, Don and I came to a certain understanding: his persona was to intimidate you with his large physique and mine was not. He knew he was the only deputy that actually knew how to be a real cop. He also knew Sheriff Dick Kienast loved the compassionate *Ki-Aikido* philosophy and that Dick had hired me to teach arrest control as well as serve as a regular patrol deputy. But Don needed proof that all this "Japanese philosophy stuff" worked in the real world.

On the first training day, I began teaching the most basic of all arrest control tactics—a wrist control technique called *sankyo*. Master Tohei first demonstrated this technique in 1953 when he considered ways to adapt *Ki-Aikido* to police work. It is a basic wristlock that can be secured from any position—it's that good. If you hold the palm of your right hand facing the ceiling and then rotate it left until it is again facing the ceiling, you will experience the immobilizing effect of this move. The twisting motion not only forces you to raise your elbow and shoulder but also raises your whole center of gravity as though you need to stand on your tiptoes. This technique is perfect for use when handcuffing "bad guys" because you can control even a large person with just one hand. That leaves your other hand free to grab your handcuffs, which are usually worn behind your back on your belt. With a good *sankyo,* you can quickly immobilize the biggest bad guy.

While Don was no bad guy, the dynamics of our first encounter were quite complex and involved a mixture of skepticism and resistance. Big Don was no dummy, and he was already familiar with this *sankyo* wristlock technique. He was preparing to resist me in the event that I tried to apply the technique on him—especially because this activity was all taking place in front of all the other deputies. Don's open resistance would enable him to pronounce his skepticism with respect to this compassionate *Ki-Aikido* stuff and the sheriff's choice to hire me.

What Don didn't know is that I was prepared to expect resistance from him. I had taken Master Tohei's *ukemi* (meaning I was the person being thrown by him) for years in the 1970s during the large public demonstrations he gave in Honolulu, up and down the West Coast, and in Japan. When he introduced and demonstrated the power of *Ki-Aikido* principles to an outsider—perhaps also a skeptic—Master Tohei always chose the biggest, baddest-looking guy in the audience. This was done by design because when the audience sees the big guy on stage being tossed around like a piece of paper, they are immediately convinced of the compassionate power of *Ki-Aikido.*

Following the lead of my teacher, I chose the big guy to demonstrate *sankyo* at the beginning of our first arrest control class. I knew it was a conflict in the making. And Master Tohei had taught me how to adjust when resistance was expected.

One of the keys to *Ki-Aikido* is that when you are deeply calm you can easily sense where another person's energy will be directed. In this case, it was obvious to me that Don was so intent on me not applying this technique in one direction that I could easily move him in the opposite direction. So when it came time for the demonstration to begin, instead of applying the *sankyo* technique, I simply reversed it to another technique called *koto oroshi*, which twisted Don's wrist 360 degrees in the opposite direction and used the powerful force of his single-minded resistance to my advantage.

All I did was respect Don's mind, power, and intention. I was then able to move with him (compassion) rather than against him (dissension). I used Don's own mighty power of resistance to throw him in a complete circle about three feet off the ground—like a piece of paper. Don landed flat on his back and looked stunned.

This state was brief, because at the precise moment his back hit the ground I lifted a little to help him bounce off the floor; then I flipped him over to his stomach. The big man was effectively pinned face down with one hand raised like a **T**, perpendicular to the floor. This position isolated his shoulder and immobilized his entire body. At this point, I very politely instructed him to put his free hand behind his back. I then proceeded to handcuff him very nicely. The big guy wasn't so big anymore.

Don was shocked, and the class was most attentive and polite from that day forward. The message it sent to Don and the deputies was that if you are deeply calm and compassionate under stressful conditions, even physically demanding conflicts, you can effectively transform the conflict into a positive outcome. This is the power of the Art of Compassion.

* * *

Many organizations fail at their initial attempts to "change the culture" and achieve meaningful performance improvement. They do so simply because employees immediately see through the so-called sincerity of senior leaders who are not personally vested and do not sustain the energy necessary to stay committed. That is, the change process only superficially involves people because they can sense the lack of sincerity, the lack of understanding of employee concerns, and the lack of commitment by members of senior leadership to actually change themselves along with everybody else.

The spiritual explanation of this common dynamic is that the typical negative energy of anxiety and fear that arose was never diffused; in truth, it was fueled by the additional negative energy of insincerity, hierarchical arrogance, and a general lack of trust. Instead of using the conflict of change to move the initiative forward with increasing energy, the conflict of change raised the negative tension and thus made it nearly impossible for the organization to sustain anything new. Old thoughts and behaviors remained.

In the process of framing organizational change, I have discovered that real change must be driven by genuine sincerity, care, and concern for all participants. Simply put, this means practicing compassion.

Real change is hard work, and people respect realism about that. In most cases, they don't mind facing the truth when the truth will help them personally. When corporate change initiatives are underscoped, underestimated, and under-resourced, employees see through the ill-conceived process. Their first reaction is, "This will never work." And it is reinforced when compassion is not present.

People instinctively know their jobs, and they know the massive effort that will be required to actually execute meaningful, lasting change. People understand intuitively the challenge of getting everyone to truly understand the realities of their own organization's work culture. When the change process is at the very beginning, there is not yet a track record of success for the initiative to have credibility in the collective mind of the employees. Since the change process does not yet have any credibility, the change process must find another driver. There is none better than compassion.

· 3 ·

THE ART OF RESPONSIBILITY

THE DILEMMA OF THE HUMAN CONDITION, said French philosopher René Descartes, is that we are infinitely free but finitely intelligent. In other words, we are completely unencumbered to make wise choices but too dumb to always know which choices are wisest—for our own good and the good of others.

To make matters worse, we cannot escape our responsibility as participants in this world. We can't just check out and do our thing because checking out has consequences like everything else. Like it or not, we all reap what we sow. And our choices always affect the bigger whole of this world we live in, for better or worse. "No man," said John Donne, "is an island, entire of itself." The same holds true in an organization.

No worker is immune from the effect of his or her own choices. And no organization is unaffected by the choices of its people. Perhaps you can see where a large problem lies for organizations. The more poor and selfish choices being made within an organization, the more conflicted an organization becomes. Eventually, getting everyone moving in the same direction is like trying to get 200 marbles to roll in a line on an asphalt road.

Widespread selfishness cannot be straightened on a superficial level—with hard-lined managing and constant redirecting. The problem is a deeper one of individual responsibility. It must therefore be addressed and remedied at a spiritual level.

Thus far, you have learned to get your organization's collective mind on the same page so that it (1) perceives organizational change as an opportunity for personal, spiritual growth, and (2) is committed to channeling the conflict of change into daily compassion. Your next challenge is to create a personal, spiritual level of accountability throughout the organization. No company, regardless of size or length of tenure, can sustain positive change unless its individuals take personal responsibility for it.

EMBODYING RESPONSIBILITY

Leading someone to take responsibility can be a difficult task but I believe it can be distilled to helping an individual embody three skills: awareness, patience, and discipline.

To introduce the most inexperienced of individuals—my children—to these skills, I created a character named "Eggaberth, the Mountain Goat," who became the hero of many bedtime stories. Eggaberth has had many life adventures on mountaintops, under the sea, and in space. But in the first stories, Eggaberth was a selfish, impatient, and undisciplined Japanese mountain goat who lived on a farm with other barnyard animals.

He ate the farmer's crops, devoured the other animals' food, and was continually bringing misery to himself and others through his own selfish actions. He couldn't see how to change his poor choices, but the farmer in the story did. This man sent Eggaberth to become an *uchi deshi* (live-in student) with my own real-life teacher, Master Koichi Tohei. There he learned how to become a responsible mountain goat able to continually adapt and improve.

The background material I used to create the Eggaberth stories was actually my own experience as an *uchi deshi* serving Master Tohei in Japan. *Uchi deshi* training is a helpful model for understanding how the Art of Responsibility enables you and your people to accept your individual role in the change process.

* * *

Since I was a foreigner, the opportunity to live with my teacher was extremely rare because the privilege was reserved for native Japanese *Ki-Aikido* students. In my case, Mr. Takashi Nonaka from Hilo, Hawaii, who was the chief instructor of the Hawaii Ki Society and a personal friend of Master Tohei, smoothed the way for me to have this unique opportunity to serve, specifically, as Master Tohei's *otomo* (personal assistant).

Otomo training is part of the regimen of an *uchi deshi* that focuses especially on the cultivation of awareness, patience, and discipline. These three qualities are the fuel for all positive change because they teach the practice of selflessness, or what Master Tohei called "emptying one's self for the greater good."

To cultivate selflessness, Master Tohei created a monastic environment for the *uchi deshi*, whereby his entire life would be sacrificed twenty-four hours a day. You sacrifice your freedom, you sacrifice your needs, you sacrifice your ego, and you practice selflessness by serving others.

As an *uchi deshi*, you live at the headquarters *dojo* (training hall) with Master Tohei. During the late 1970s when I lived at headquarters, there were seven *uchi deshi,* including me. The seven of us slept on the floor and lived in one room above the *dojo*; it is very difficult training to say the least. Everyday and at every moment the life of the *uchi deshi* could be turned upside down.

We had already sacrificed our freedom upon admission into this twenty-four-hour-a-day monastic environment, and thus we had office duties, cleaning duties, and special training classes to attend, as well as classes that we were responsible for teaching. The primary point of the training was that we were to be completely unattached to any selfish motivation, completely available to serve the greater good, and always prepared to change our direction, our anticipated schedule, and our responsibilities at any given moment.

If Master Tohei said the plan of the day was changing, then we had to adjust immediately. To meet the needs of the moment, we were taught to move on the first letter *I* of the Japanese word *Ima* which means "now." In order to do this, your mind had to be fully aware such that you were always ready to adapt to new conditions. Anything less than a swift response would mean that your mind or your consciousness was late. This mental awareness is a must in the martial art of *Ki–Aikido*. The aim is to be so calm and aware of your surroundings that your mind is like a mirror. In this state, you can react very quickly as if your attacker is moving in slow motion. You can clearly "see" the conflict rising and immediately make adjustments to transform the circumstance into a positive outcome.

In an organizational setting, I like to call this practice of awareness a *responsible reflex*. It is personified when each individual in your organization approaches everyday circumstances with an awareness that, at any given moment, a need might hang in the balance. If the need is met, the change moves forward in a positive direction. If the need is passed off, ignored, or put off, the change moves backward. You can see that the more the needs of the moment are met, the easier it is to maintain the momentum of change.

Otomo training is also a great model for learning patience and discipline. Your role as *otomo* is simply to anticipate the needs of the moment. Early each day someone would be assigned as Master Tohei's *otomo*. The training is to assist him in whatever he is doing, wherever he is going (you travel with him), and to do so without calling attention to yourself. Your aim is to be invisible in your selflessness. This type of training is exhausting to your consciousness, as you must pay constant attention to every interaction and every nuance; however, you must do so without staring and without making Master Tohei or those around him feel uncomfortable. Doing so requires great patience and discipline.

Your *otomo* duties include everything from taking Master Tohei's *ukemi* (that is, being thrown as his partner when he teaches) to driving his car as chauffeur; pouring tea when visitors arrive for meetings; preparing, packing, and carrying his luggage; helping him dress; and proactively and silently (and preferably invisibly) attending to his every need. All this must be done seamlessly by anticipating the need and performing the service without being asked and without calling attention to yourself. Again, this is a responsible reflex that requires great patience and self-discipline.

ANTICIPATING NEEDS

My favorite example of *otomo* awareness, patience, and discipline is the need to watch Master Tohei's eyes. Suppose Master Tohei is sitting at his writing desk at the back end of the office. A postal employee brings in the day's mail and sets it on the counter near the entrance door. Master Tohei simply glances at the bundle of mail. Such is his intention. If I am aware, I should—without being asked—attend immediately to the four things that I have learned already. These four things should be done in sequence, they should be performed smoothly, and the overall process should start moving invisibly on the N of the word "Now."

These are the four activities:

1. *Swiftly, yet calmly, pick up the bundle of mail without calling attention to myself.*

2. *Go to the special drawer near Master Tohei's writing desk, which contains his reading glasses.*

3. *Go to yet another desk that has another special drawer that contains the Master's favorite letter opener.*

4. *Collect all three items and place them neatly in front of the Master.*

This sequence of activities is but one small example of selfless attention where the training focus is to give up all of my needs; instead, I exercise the awareness, patience, and discipline necessary to be responsible for others' needs twenty-four hours a day. If Master Tohei had to ask me to collect these four things, or if I hesitated, delegated, or ignored them, then I would be scolded (which he did) for not being responsible. It would also mean losing face for not executing my duty at the high level the Master required and for which I was supposed to be capable.

The only way to manage this kind of twenty-four-hour-a-day pressure is to accept the highest notion of responsibility. In other words, the moment you become excessively attached to personal needs is the same moment you invite a lack of awareness, and a level of selfish irresponsibility, that hinders behaviors that serve the greater needs of the initiative.

As I have alluded to, the Art of Responsibility was taught with such high standards to the *uchi deshi* because the martial art of *Ki-Aikido* requires you to literally anticipate your attacker's move by feeling his negative energy, or *Ki*, coming toward you. If you do not anticipate this, you are late in your reaction and at great risk. This type of all-consuming *otomo* training has the cumulative effect of training you to "see" things through your extension of *Ki* and not necessarily through your physical eyes alone.

Otomo training is the ultimate standard of personal responsibility for any organization. Practicing such a high level of awareness and selflessness teaches ongoing patience because the people you serve control the tempo of all action. It also teaches unbending self-discipline because you learn to continually redirect your own needs and desires in the service of a greater good. You become invisible, so to speak, in order to remain aware of the ever-changing needs around you. In this place, you are able to adjust, adapt, and act immediately in the most responsible way possible.

When you and your people empty yourselves completely in this manner, you will each begin to taste the real depth of possibility for making a difference in an organization. Another way to look at it is that all individuals in your organization begin to see themselves like the parts of a human body—inextricably connected to and responsible for maintaining the health of the whole.

The Truest Form of Accountability Is Personal Responsibility

Anchoring the notion that employees take responsibility for their actions is fundamental to both change management and spiritual development. Let me begin by clarifying my purposeful use of the term *responsibility* as opposed to the often-used word in business, *accountability*.

I believe accountability is important, but I use the word *responsibility* to frame this third Art for a very important reason. The word *accountability* often denotes a senior manager's frame of reference or perspective. It tends to point to the senior person holding a subordinate (per the organizational hierarchy) to his word, or to the budget, or to the operational plan, or to the planned forecast.

Don't get me wrong, I am all for this kind of accountability. But when you instead refer to *responsibility* the connotation is individual: "I am responsible." This ensures the spiritual motivation for doing what you say comes from within you; it is not forced or lorded upon you from higher up the organizational hierarchy. From the correct frame of reference, people want to take responsibility because, in the language of spiritual development, they are practicing the important and basic human value of being true to your word. No one outside yourself needs to tell you what to do or hold you accountable as if you would run astray without someone standing over you.

This perspective is so critical because people must be self-motivated to do what is necessary at any given moment in order for the process to sustain momentum. It is necessary because if you say you will deliver X, Y, or Z against this budget, this operating plan, or this forecast, then you hold yourself personally responsible to fulfill your promises without excuses.

In a competitive business environment that requires multiple deliverables to be executed across the organization in order to achieve planned results, every individual must be counted upon to deliver. Any failure to do what you say you will derail the efforts of an entire company that is depending upon the successful delivery of every piece of the puzzle. No measurable and sustainable performance improvement can take place if the left or right hand of the enterprise cannot be counted upon to deliver.

THE LAW OF CAUSATION AND APPLICATION OF THE ART OF RESPONSIBILITY

Observing businesses that perform poorly is a lot like observing children who grow up spoiled and unruly because they have not learned about positive and negative consequences at home. When children and grown-ups are led to believe that it does not seem to matter whether you do what you say you will, then people, young and old, tend not to perform up to promised expectations.

In a changing business environment, you should expect people to perform to the best of their ability—but only if they are given the tools to succeed. If managers, operators, salespeople, or even CEOs are protected by an ineffective and undisciplined board of directors, a "good ol' boy" network, a poor performance appraisal system, or a culture where performance and rewards are not tightly coupled, then you have a basic breakdown in individual responsibility.

Earlier we posed the question, "How do you know when the culture is changing?" This is an important question because of the difficulty in seeing a positive change in the culture. Therefore, because we cannot see the collective mind of the company, change is first observed in a change of collective behavior.

I have found that if an organization focuses on behavior, then an entire new world opens up to everyone. Visibility and clarity are enhanced and the Art of Responsibility gains firm footing because there is something to hold up as the standard of behavior. While your people must understand the new initiative and buy into it on a spiritual level (the first two Arts), there will still be inconsistency in the initiative if the people do not also have a clear and visible model for their behavior. Only then can they be expected to hold themselves personally responsible.

So, successful change requires tight alignment between measurable behavior, the change strategy, and the annual operating plan. If people do not know exactly what to do (i.e., actions to be performed in order to meet the plan) as well as how to do it (i.e., behaviors that evidence company values), then you cannot possibly sustain your ability to execute change—there is no standard of what it means to be *responsible*.

In this context, clarity is power. People can make themselves personally responsible to perform when they know what counts, and leaders can thus hold them responsible for doing what they say. Then—and only then—can you create a high-performance culture with staying power. This is where the application of the Art of Responsibility comes into play.

When proper action and consequences are fairly and tightly

coupled, it means there is clarity, consistency, and, perhaps most importantly, predictability. Applying the Art of Responsibility is about designing practices that will help you to create a sustainable high-performance culture characterized by consistency and predictability. In order to effectively lead the performance improvement process, rewards as well as negative consequences must be applied in a consistent and predictable manner throughout the enterprise.

CREATING A RESPONSIBILITY STANDARD AT DURACELL

Let's get very specific. Many leaders know that cultural change is related to focusing upon *what* we do (action plans) as well as *how* we work (living the company values). But change initiatives often fail because the leaders of change fail to get detailed and individually specific about the whats and the hows.

When working with a large organization, I like to choose the worst performers to start a company-wide change process because a successful turnaround in the worst areas of the business can then be leveraged—held up as a standard—to motivate the rest of the company.

For example, Duracell was experiencing serious quality problems in one of its product portfolios. This particular product was sold into the company's original equipment manufacturers (OEM) business serving the electronics industry, including camera manufacturers in Japan. The quality problems were becoming so bad that the electronics and camera manufacturers were placing embarrassing preprinted notes inside the camera packages encouraging consumers to replace the "portable power components" (batteries) of the camera with other brands. (The OEMs could not merely stop sourcing from my client because of contractual obligations.)

Duracell has a world-class market presence and reputation for high quality. The bigger problem for the giant was that it is a highly visible merchandiser of consumer products with multiple product lines that sold through the same channels in which the camera products sold. So, while the Wal-Marts, Kmarts, and Home Depots of the world sold a lot of Duracell products directly to the consumer, the same places also sold photo and other battery-powered electronic equipment in their stores. These OEM camera and electronic equipment manufacturers were being sourced poor product, thus giving the rest of Duracell's product lines a bad quality rap by simple association. And, while the OEM business was not significant in terms of revenue to Duracell's bottom line, the poor quality of this particular battery business unit was causing a significant brand image problem. While the quality of the alkaline products sold directly to the consumer were first rate, the quality problems with their specialty products sold to the OEMs could bring down the high-quality reputation of the entire company. It was the classic "only as strong as the weakest link" scenario playing out.

Since the entire Duracell company was going through a significant cultural change process already, we decided to turn our focus on changing the culture of the manufacturing plant that was producing the poor-quality product. In this way, we could create dramatic performance improvement where it was needed most and subsequently stave off any major brand disasters.

Together we accomplished the needed change in a very short time frame. The centerpiece was working to create a high-performance culture where everyone would take responsibility by "thinking and acting like owners" and "choosing to make a difference."

After only eight months into the change process, David Bluestein, then-president of Duracell USA, visited the manufacturing plant at the request of Ed Battocchio, senior vice president (SVP) of Manufacturing and Technical Operations. After his visit, David wrote the following note to the senior total quality manager of the plant.

> Again, thanks to you and your staff for an informative and encouraging visit to your manufacturing facility. Tremendous progress has been made in the last eight months on all key fronts and measures!!! There is no question in my mind that your facility is now equal among its peer USA plants. Many of us would not have expected this result so quickly. I look forward to continued progress and further outstanding results. You and your team should be very proud.

Here are some of the measurable performance improvement results that were quickly achieved and sustained:

- Safety performance
    - *84 percent reduction in OSHA recordables*
    - *87 percent improvement in Lost Work Time Injuries*
- Customer service
    - *100 percent on-time delivery*
- Supplier quality percent nonconformance
    - *47 percent improvement*
- Quality—visual leakage
    - *99.8 percent improvement*
- Lithium—customer returns
    - *100 percent improvement*
- Zinc Air—customer returns
    - *99 percent improvement*
- Temporary engineering deviations
    - *80 percent improvement (Zinc Air)*
    - *76 percent improvement (Lithium)*
- Employee turnover rate
    - *47 percent improvement*

These results came because everyone at the plant learned the importance of the Art of Responsibility.

Recognizing and Rewarding
the Right Stuff

The secret to our success was in the simplicity of an approach grounded in three basic activities:

1. *Build upon the good things.*

2. *Get rid of the non-valued.*

3. *Uncover the unpleasant obstacles that are really holding people back.*

The following steps were taken in support of the three activities. Together the following steps established a new level of personal responsibility that was based on knowledge of what was expected, what was rewarded, and how both were expected to be executed. By applying these same steps you can also lead your organization or specific team to adopt the Art of Responsibility:

1. *Interview everyone confidentially about the good, bad, and ugly.* The approach at Duracell began with a thorough interview process. I gained critical information from every person in the plant regarding what they felt were key obstacles to peak performance and what they felt was working well and should remain unchanged. I make it a point never to editorialize what people are telling me in an interview. I don't probe or lead their answers; I simply listen to the unchallenged perceptions of the interviewees. My job is to learn, not evaluate, at this point in

the process. It may take many months of interviews, but when I am through, I can summarize the feedback into actionable themes that represent the largest majority. In these large representations, I can protect confidentiality and still uncover the key issues that inhibit positive change. The end result of such an interview process is the ability to discover the real cultural issues that prohibit everyone from working to the best of their ability. If you listen well in this interview process, it is possible to capture even the most sensitive issues that inhibit personal responsibility and team development.

2. *Create action plans from feedback.* With the information from the collective interviews, the senior management and I developed action plans that focused on the highest frequency issues that occurred across all functions. Follow-through is the key in this step. There has to be a concerted effort to face obstacles head on and thus free everyone in the organization to make a greater contribution to the process of performance improvement. The mere fact that each employee has the opportunity to voice his or her perceptions for a full hour during the interview phase makes the follow-through work infinitely more effective. In fact, the entire process is driven by the employees themselves; employees at every desk, on every machine, and in every lab are put into a position to be the real performance improvement heroes.

3. *Establish plantwide target behaviors.* The senior management team was asked to custom-design a list of target behaviors from

the feedback action steps. These would be the particular behaviors that epitomized a commitment to replacing the negative behaviors that were identified as obstacles to peak performance. As we all know, words and promises to change the culture are difficult to live up to, especially if there is a history of unacceptable behavior. In order to maximize the likelihood of sustainable change, a focus upon actual target behaviors helps everyone remain committed to the change process. That is, because people can visibly observe the positive results of the behavioral cogs of the change, they remain committed. Success breeds success.

4. *Lead according to target behaviors.* Accordingly, the senior management team at Duracell began to lead the cultural change and performance improvement process. The first step was drafting a list of plant-specific target behaviors (see the following sidebar) and then practicing them immediately themselves. By doing so, the entire interview population observed through the visible behaviors of their leaders that (1) senior management heard and respected the performance improvement interview feedback and (2) senior management was willing to begin the process of creating a new plant culture in order to improve performance. The sidebar shows the actual list drawn up by the plant.

PLANT-SPECIFIC BEST TARGET BEHAVIORS

The New Plant TRIAD:
Safety, Quality, Customer Service:

1.

All Jobs Start with Safety.

2.

Celebrate Successes, Big or Small—Praise People Daily.

3.

Help Each Other—Look beyond Your Department—Focus on Plant Success.

4.

We Are a Team—Open Lines of Communication Are a Must.

5.

Talk about It Openly—Silence Accomplishes Nothing.

6.

Disagreement Is Healthy—Resolution Is Necessary.

7.

Respond Professionally to Differences—Make Bulletproof a Reality.

(continues on next page)

(continued from previous page)

8.
WHAT *Is Right . . . Not* **WHO** *Is Right.*

9.
Improve Meetings Every Day—Remember the Five Ws.

10.
Manage the Risks, Make Mistakes, Learn.

11.
Take Responsibility and Follow Through—Choose to Make a Difference.

12.
Create Our Future with Your **BEST** *Actions Today.*

Mission

Safely Produce Quality Products to Meet Customer Needs, Helping Duracell Become the Leading Consumer Battery Company in the World.

Keep in mind that target behaviors are simply specific opportunities for individual responsibility. The difference is that they are employee generated and therefore motivated from a spiritual place inside each person. This is an entirely different place from which to inspire new behavior from people. And it is the essence of the effectiveness of the Art of Responsibility.

Accountability through Community

In a spiritual community—a church, for instance—people give feedback to people who are not walking the talk or living the values. Organizational change in business requires the same candor and level of responsibility. The key is to first establish the standards of behavior and make them clear to everyone in the community. In this manner, no one is immune from reaping the seeds he or she has sown. But also everyone takes success and failure more personally, because in every case the community actually reaps positive or negative results from seeds that have been sown. Therefore, there exists both a causal, personal accountability and a corporate accountability. And the corporate accountability is not based upon hierarchy but rather is the result of the good, responsible actions of every caring member of the community.

The sum total to practicing the Art of Responsibility is an emphasis on personal integrity and personal responsibility in order to create a do-what-you-say culture. With a focus on personal responsibility less emphasis needs to be given to the traditional notion of accountability, which most employees interpret negatively. There were initially, for example, senior executives at Duracell headquarters (Bethel, Connecticut) and the Research and Development Center (Needham, Massachusetts) screaming at the Specialty Plant management team to improve quality and change the culture. The problem was that the people at the plant did not know how to change the culture. They could not "own" the change process. That all changed when we implemented the

Art of Responsibility into the plant. Change suddenly became personal—and therefore "ownable."

* * *

Each year, world-class performers in sports or the arts expect to get better. If you do not, you are falling behind the competition. Expecting higher performance of yourself is a good thing, and it is the only way an organization will move from being inspired to change to actually enacting change.

In fact, those I have seen rise to the occasion and lead change at work are those who approach the cultural change challenge as a *calling*, as though it has spiritual significance. I believe the change process is just that important, because it serves as a wonderful occasion to put into practice the best human values every day. It should be refreshing to know that practicing the behaviors that you know are right are the exact same behaviors that lead to the very best performance for individuals, teams, companies, and spiritual communities. This is the essence of the Art of Responsibility: helping individuals discover the behaviors they know are right and that will move the company toward the change it desires.

THE ART OF RELAXATION

I FIRST EXPERIENCED THE CRITICAL IMPORTANCE of this fourth Art as a young downhill ski racer. My coach was a Frenchman named Jean-Pierre Pascal. In the early 1970s, he invited me to live with him and his wife, Helenka, at their home in Squaw Valley, California. It would be the setting for a major life lesson.

Jean-Pierre lead the Olympic Valley USA Ski Team of which I was a member. The team traveled extensively looking for the best snow so we could train year round. We skied the famous slopes surrounding Lake Tahoe from the late fall through April then Red Lodge, Montana, and Val Thorens, France, in May and June, where the high-altitude glaciers retained snow despite the summer heat. At the high altitudes, we focused our training on the slalom events. Then in July and August, we would travel to Argentina where it was winter. There we would focus exclusively on the longest event of all—the downhill. It was my favorite—the faster, the better. It was also a perfect metaphor for the high-stakes corporate pressure I would later help organizations negotiate.

COOL UNDER PRESSURE

In an international downhill race you typically go over three miles from start to finish in less than three minutes. Factoring in the slow start out of the gate, you are easily averaging over 60 miles per hour (mph). In some World Cup Downhill courses you top 90 mph at the finish. Up to about 45 mph, you feel in control. Above that speed, a new feeling arises. You are a passenger on a pair of thin, fast-moving planks. You feel as though you are floating and so to feel the skis on the snow you have to learn to relax your entire upper body.

You cannot simply turn or stop at will above 45 mph. The race becomes more like a swift dance as you constantly search for ways to bend with the mountain's curves to maintain stability and produce more speed. If you tense up in this scenario, your ski edges chatter and grab the snow, decreasing your speed and adding precious seconds to your time.

To excel during the three-minute blur, you must above all relax and fix your eyes far ahead of your present position. You must maintain "your line," or path of descent, in order to properly position yourself as you enter the most treacherous sections of the course. Once your speed exceeds 80 mph, if you lose your balance and stick out an arm, the force of the wind can toss you sideways and into a perilous, high-speed tumble.

My downhill trainer was yet another Frenchman named Philippe Mollard, a former FIS (Federation of International Skiing) World Downhill Champion. I was young and impressionable and would do anything to become a world-class downhiller, so I hung on every tip he offered. Philippe's first piece of advice was to do things scarier than our chosen discipline. Even when we were "free skiing" with Philippe at our training center at Squaw Valley at Lake Tahoe, he would constantly remind us that "if you are not seeing the whites of your own eyes three times a day," then you are not preparing (scaring) yourself for faster, improved performance. It was his way of encouraging us to relax in the midst of these highly stressful situations.

My fellow downhillers and I took his advice to heart and began to experiment with other high-stakes sports like rock climbing in the Alps, skydiving over Lake Tahoe, and speed skiing at over 100 mph. We learned that Philippe was correct. Exposing ourselves to new experiences helped us be at peace with the dangers of downhill racing with which we were much more familiar. We had learned a key lesson of the Art of Relaxation: when the stakes are high, your inner strength is far more important than your outer strength.

Downhillers cannot out-muscle the forces of momentum and gravity. We had to find our inner strength to keep us physically relaxed, emotionally calm, and mentally focused. This was the only way to finish the race successfully and in one piece.

This inner strength had two critical effects:

1. *It allowed us to perform at the highest level with real focus.*

2. *It kept us adaptable to constant, even unexpected, changes.*

The importance of both roles became crystal clear to me during one very close call. Even today, I am reminded that the Art of Relaxation did more than help me stay on course; it literally saved my life. It has since saved the lives of many businesses in similar perilous conditions. If there is one tool you must possess in the midst of the tough conditions or threatening competition, it is the ability to relax and focus on what matters most.

Prepared for the Unexpected

In Argentina in the early 1970s, Juan Perón was in power, and the Americans were not in good graces. Military guards with machine guns were stationed outside every one of our hotel rooms. This not only put a damper on our nightlife, it was also very unnerving.

It was mid-August and in preparation for an upcoming race in September, we were skiing our legs into shape by flying from the top to the bottom of the mountain without stopping, over and over. Our coaches would stand at various sections of the racecourse, videotape us, and then radio their feedback to the other coaches standing strategically at other critical sections of the course. Each night, we would watch the film shot during the day and listen to the coaches' audiotaped comments.

There was a purpose behind all this. Memorizing the racecourse was a critical preparation step. Because you often cannot see around the next turn or over the next pitch during a race, you must memorize your preferred line of descent. This "line," as we called it, is the optimal place to position yourself throughout the entire course. It allows you to safely and swiftly negotiate the dangerous terrain at 80 to 90 mph.

There was always one hitch, however. Racecourses always changed—slightly so from new tracks laid down by the skiers preceding your descent throughout the day, and significantly so after a big snow.

To minimize these changes, a lot of attention is paid to properly and continually grooming World Cup racecourses so they do not break farther apart as each successive racer shreds down the course. Large diesel Caterpillars are used in North America and Europe for this purpose. The method is especially handy when fresh powder falls the night before. The new snow is easily and quickly compacted before the race takes place, which keeps the course in much the same condition as when the skiers prepared. It was a different story in the southern hemisphere.

In Bariloche, Argentina, there were no diesel Caterpillars for grooming. Instead, the Argentine military would "boot-pack" the course. Seventy military men in tall boots were ordered to walk straight up the racecourse, packing down two feet of fresh powder with nothing more than the strength of their legs. They would stomp down the new snow and re-create what was, the day before, our icy-fast racetrack. To make matters worse, after the boot-packing came "side-slipping." The same seventy soldiers would don their skis and sidestep down the course to re-create a (supposedly) smooth surface.

The obvious problem was that all that stomping and side-stepping from men greatly varying in weight and leg strength significantly changed the racecourse terrain.

At the end of this particular Argentine racecourse, you would come to a steep downhill pitch that could significantly increase your speed to the finish. To take advantage of the pitch we called "the waterfall," skiers needed to avoid catapulting into the air at the crest. Instead, the goal was to land quickly on the downhill side of the waterfall and tuck tightly to the finish.

To avoid sailing off the crest, you had to pre-jump it. Doing so required raising yourself off the ground just before reaching the crest of the waterfall. When the pre-jump was properly executed, you safely dropped over the waterfall and hugged the steep pitch to the finish line. Relaxation was key because you couldn't see your landing spot. And on this particular course, most of the waterfall—the "underhill," as we called it—was an extremely dangerous washboard of bumpy terrain. The ideal (and only safe) landing spot was right down the middle of the waterfall where the course was smooth and fast.

The day before I was to race, the perfect "line" leading to this invisible alley had been marked exactly twenty feet left of a flag gate that was placed on the right side of the course at the lip of the waterfall. Pre-jumping at this mark was essential. The exact spatial position for executing the pre-jump successfully was fixed in my memory of the course the days before . . . when it hadn't yet snowed.

After an all-night snowstorm that added two feet of new snow, the Argentine army went out the following morning to boot-pack and side-slip the course, temporarily removing the flag gates and then returning them where they thought they had previously been. I was soon to learn that no amount of anticipation or visualization was enough to prepare me for the changes I would be forced to negotiate.

I was the third racer scheduled in a format where we would leave the starting gate in one-minute intervals—normally plenty of time for each finishing racer to get out of the way for the next racer to finish. I was standing in the starting gate ready to take off, and racer number one was already well down the course. However, the critically important right-hand gate at the crest of the waterfall had not been returned to its original location by the Argentine military. As I stood waiting for the countdown to start my time, the first racer had flown over the crest and skied right into the washboard underhill terrain at 80-plus mph. He blew right out of his skis and crashed his broken body into the scoreboard located at the finish line.

Coaches had immediately radioed word of the serious injury to officials at the starting gate and instructed them to stop all racers from coming down the course. Unfortunately, by the time they did so, racer number two was already halfway down the course, and I had just left the starting gate. I was completely unaware of the dreadful conditions ahead of me as I screamed down the course.

Racer number two also failed to pre-jump at the right location and catapulted himself into the dangerous washboard terrain. His skis exploded out from under him, and the razor-sharp edge of one ski sliced open the inside of his left knee like a sushi chef cutting sashimi. As I unknowingly approached the crest of the waterfall at about 80 mph, racer number two was lying on the washboard terrain in a heap of pulsating blood; racer number one was still wrapped around the scoreboard.

At the last second, I caught a blurry glimpse of coaches, spectators, and Argentine soldiers waving furiously from both sides of the course. I intuitively knew I could not just turn sideways and stop, so I gently straightened my upper body into the force of wind. Doing so allowed me to gradually slow down from my 80 mph pace. I knew there was certain danger ahead, but the Art of Relaxation kicked in. Like the first two racers, I hit what was now clearly an incorrect mark at the top of the waterfall and hurled into the washboard where my fallen compatriots were laying. But I had centered myself embracing the wind on my chest as a brake, I relaxed my upper body completely, and then I managed to negotiate the treacherous bumps with my knees pounding my chest. At approximately 50 mph I flew by and narrowly missed one fellow ski racer who was lying in a pool of red snow. I was then (with a prayer) able to adjust, negotiate the scoreboard, and avoid the same fate as the first racer. I survived, but the margin of survival was extremely slight. The only real difference between me and my fellow racers was a quick visual cue and an ability to relax under pressure. On that day, in those conditions, the Art of Relaxation was a lifesaver.

THE DIFFERENCE BETWEEN GOOD AND BAD STRESS

The business world—and, frankly, the universe itself—is changing all the time. It is in a state of constant flux. At every moment, your organization is in a much better position to succeed if it learns to relax, expect the unexpected, and trust that the collective inner (spiritual) strength of the people is your best resource. You probably don't need to be reminded that when individuals, divisions, or entire companies come under severe stress, they lose focus and cannot perform to their highest potential. In fact, significant organizational stress causes personal and team performance to move backward. While you might be able to "shock" people to briefly perform in a crisis, short-term upticks in performance come at great sacrifice and much personal pain. They are not, therefore, sustainable.

Long-term, high-performance cultures require clear and tangible behavioral standards (the Art of Responsibility) that allow people to relax, focus, and deliver results on a consistent basis. In such high-performance cultures, there are few "crises." Instead, there are "challenges" that are interpreted as opportunities to improve using the existing skills of clarity, visibility, and focus.

Most business executives raise their eyebrows when I bring up this fourth Art. The notion of relaxation seems inconsistent with the driving force of performance improvement. But these are not mutually exclusive activities. When I explain the Art of Relaxation to change leaders I often do so by simply saying that in every great performance, inner strength drives outer performance. It is not difficult to get buy-in on this thought as all business leaders have seen the aftermath of someone (perhaps themselves) choking under pressure. That choking, I explain, is a lack of inner strength—a lack of a relaxed inner foundation that caused the outer performance to be less than peak.

An easy metaphor that illustrates the difference between an organization that applies the Art of Relaxation and one that does not is the difference between a regular egg and a hard-boiled egg. Drop the regular egg from a mere two feet (hardly "high" stakes) and the whole thing splats into a gooey mess. No more egg. Drop the hard-boiled egg from two feet and it will crack or dent the shell but the body of the egg remains intact. So the metaphor goes that those companies that have trained themselves to react to high stakes with a collective inner strength—with relaxed clarity, focus, and visibility—are able to remain intact.

Replacing Distress with Eustress

So often, the highest stakes that employees feel are external pressures imposed by senior management who supposedly are encouraging them to perform. Although a certain amount of tension is useful for the promotion of a high-performance, execution-oriented culture, most change leaders confuse good tension with bad tension . . . what psychologists call *eustress* and *distress,* respectively.

Eustress is a positive and focused self-imposed pressure that helps you consistently deliver the planned results. With the right amount of eustress, you can maintain high energy, despite external conditions, because of the "self-imposed" desire to excel. Eustress is the spiritual energy that makes people want to be the best they can be, and it is synonymous with a person's will to win. In short, it is at the heart of self-motivation.

Distress, on the other hand, is debilitating to peak performance. When you are distressed, you lose focus and perform poorly because you do not have a self-imposed will to excel—you are simply succumbing to other people's external expectations. In the world of business, if you did not sign up for the objective or task, if your deliverables are perceived by you to be unrealistic, then you are operating out of somebody else's belief system.

The Art of Relaxation is characterized by replacing the debilitating distress (i.e., external pressure and expectations) in your organization with empowering eustress (i.e., internal drive and responsibility).

To do so for a change initiative, it is critical to secure buy-in for each individual's performance results. When people are forced to accept performance expectations they believe are unrealistic, they will lack the inner strength to calmly deal with the pressure of executing those deliverables. They will experience far more distress than eustress.

Another common scenario that gives rise to company-wide distress is an unfocused and reactive business culture. If employees believe management is constantly changing the game on them and adding new deliverables without taking old initiatives off their agendas, they will not relax under the pressure to perform. Without reprioritizing and clarifying the operational to-do list and then allowing people to focus on clear strategic priorities, you will kill people's internal motivation.

These two most common scenarios—(1) forced acceptance and accountability and (2) an unfocused and reactive culture—can easily be avoided by applying the Art of Relaxation to a company. Replacing collective distress with collective eustress happens when the leaders of change provide three specific conditions at all levels of the organization:

1. *Clarity of purpose.* When the business strategy and behavioral expectations are crystal clear to everyone (not unlike the ideal "line" on a racing course), each person can relax and draw from an internal drive to succeed, instead of being driven by external expectations from stressed superiors.

2. *Focus of requirements.* All workers must know what is specifically required of them in order for the initiative to succeed. This condition is different than behavioral expectations, and it is more than "just do your job." You must provide each individual a critical to-do list—a verbal or written one—that details the most important tasks to be accomplished each day. When you do so, the initiative can gain momentum and be sustained.

3. *Visibility of progress.* When the core operating metrics are made available for everyone to see and track, the whole company is further motivated from the inside out. They then can see that what they are doing is progressing the company's efforts. This

condition is critical in order for people to sustain peak performance—without seeing that their extra efforts are worthwhile, they will be tempted to back off the throttle.

Under these conditions, business peak performance plays out no differently than athletic peak performance. Individuals can go about their days with an inner strength and calmness capable of producing extraordinary results in less-than-ideal circumstances.

THE SWEET SPOT OF PEAK PERFORMANCE

When I introduce these three conditions to executives, managers, and employees throughout an organization trying to change, I use experienced-based training. This allows participants to understand for themselves how one's inner strength (or lack thereof) affects the ability to perform. When you directly experience for yourself how a calm, clear, and focused inner state gives you tremendous strength of action, you immediately become a believer in the power of the Art of Relaxation.

A basic truism of peak performance is that "you are stronger when you are relaxed." For example, tense one of your hands right now wherever you are sitting. Spread out your fingers, and make your hand and wrist really tight; see the veins, muscles, and tendons in your hand stand out. Now, with your hand in this tense position, shake it back and forth as fast as you can. Note your experience.

Now, as a contrast to that experience, completely relax your hand, fingers, and wrist. Once again, shake your hand back and forth as rapidly as possible. Which is faster? Of course, the relaxed hand is much faster. Any performer knows that this relaxed state is the sweet spot of peak performance.

Do you remember your physics? Force = Mass × Acceleration. Can you change the mass of your hand? Of course not. But you can change the acceleration of your hand. And you just did so in greater measure by relaxing it. You thus experienced that you have greater focus and force of strength through a relaxed state than through a tense one.

I usually spend a half day helping participants experience for themselves the power of a relaxed and focused inner self, or spirit. The wow factor is high as the participant's previous belief system is shattered by a sort of Jack Welch "boundarylessness" experience (as made famous by General Electric's commitment to innovation, training, and leadership development). When people have a true encounter with their greater potential through relaxation, they often come to a realization that their life up to that point has been functioning with a self-imposed emergency brake on. When the brake is suddenly off the collective spirit of the people, an organization's performance can ramp up quickly.

Relaxing the Whole Organization

I recently sat down with a client's CEO after my Assessment Phase (the Art of Preparation) had been completed, and it was not a cheery conversation. There was an enormous lack of focus, which was causing widespread distress, wasted energy, and poor performance. I had created a bubble chart to demonstrate the lack of clarity and visible metrics that were the primary causes. Bubbles were all over the place, and few were truly connected. I then had the unpleasant task of asking the CEO to look at the organization from the perspective of a middle manager—looking up the organization at all the confusion being created by multiple vice presidents championing their own independent initiatives in different parts of the organization.

My bubble chart showed multiple bubbles (representing the independent initiatives) floating around an ill-defined space (the organization). I told the CEO three things would be required for any of the bubbled initiatives to actually help the company in the long run: clarity, focus, and visibility. At that moment, the large organization possessed none of the three.

In fact, two different senior vice presidents (SVPs) were telling the company their change initiative was the most important in company history (IT and Sales & Marketing). Not only that, but they had separately hired two different consulting firms to help drive those initiatives. And a third SVP (of Operations), who had 80 percent of the company employees reporting to him, set out to hire two more consulting companies (1) to reduce variability and improve quality through six sigma (a quality-focused consulting firm), as well as (2) to teach "lean manufacturing principles," drive out waste (*muda*), and completely change operations to a format of dedicated cell production lines that would completely blow apart existing manufacturing organizational structures (another lean-focused consulting firm). And finally, the vice president of Organizational Development was leading change with company-wide HR initiatives (and, yes, additional consultants) that worked through the company "university."

Unraveling the Tension

All this would be laughable if it were not so common. Everyone has good intentions, everyone is driving for results, everyone is working hard . . . but the people caught in the cross-fire think senior leadership has completely lost touch with reality. The various change leaders often initiate so much simultaneous change that during a season when the company thinks it is taking steps to secure a better future, it is actually sinking into severe distress.

When it gets to that point—and many companies get there—the confusion and distress is so great that people shut up, spirits tense up, politics ramp up, and fears rise up. In this environment, everything is happening so fast that people start flailing off the deep end—the waterfall, if you will—and end up in a heap at the bottom of the mountain of work. It happens every day in companies across the country. And it's completely avoidable.

In our example above, what was the remedy for the seriously conflicted company? It isn't rocket science. The Art of Relaxation required that the various grand change initiatives driven by the well-intended senior leaders be aligned, simplified, and prioritized. Doing so would create the clarity, focus, and visibility necessary for company-wide peak performance.

With the bubble chart in hand, I told the CEO how we could merge all these freely floating bubbles under his central leadership.

First, we would do away with all the fancy pet names that each senior leader had given his or her initiatives. Instead, the CEO and I would create and lead a single change initiative that would align each of the senior leader's critical functions with a single set of visible company-wide metrics.

We did so and thus clarified the various initiatives into one initiative championed by the CEO himself.

Second, we would instruct everyone to stop performing any task that was done out of routine, habit, or history.

We did so and thus gave every employee instant, focused power to only do things that added value to the new initiative going forward. We encouraged all employees to take everything nonstrategic off their to-do list and quickly rid the company of much of its distress. In essence, we set the people up for relaxed, sustainable performance improvement.

Finally, we would create a single set of four cross-functional performance metrics for the entire company that could be tracked on a daily basis. The measures would indicate whether or not the collective actions of the company were moving in the desired direction.

We did so and thus created measurable, visible results that were tied to annual performance reviews and compensation benefits. We simplified daily to-dos by measuring and rewarding the right stuff. The core metrics showed, visibly, that not only was the new strategy being executed but also employees' work was making a measurable difference. We taught everyone how each metric worked, how it was calculated, what deliverables it measured, and how each person's job affected the company's progress. Every employee gained a "line of sight" for navigating his or her daily work "course" with high effectiveness.

* * *

When applied in concert, the above three measures quickly removed the collective distress and replaced it with a collective eustress that was capable of sustaining significant, measurable performance improvement. People began to operate out of a relaxed inner strength and execution was significantly better. In the end, the company exceeded their goals in less than five years. The private equity firm that owned the company had invested in *people* and created value (Human Capital Index), increasing "the multiple" of the company's value. All this value was created simply by growing and developing every employee while simultaneously enhancing the quality of everyone's life *at work*. In addition, every employee's future was secured (even in the American textile industry) as the firm was sold to another American-based company desiring to leverage and expand the kind of culture we had created. The new parent company was going to vertically integrate, acquire a valued supplier (my client), and was owned by Warren Buffett's Berkshire Hathaway Fund.

Every employee's future was now going to be secured instead of being outsourced. It would seem that developing people with clarity, visibility, and focus as the centerpiece of strategy is also good for business!

Relax and Win

There have been many other stories that have proven to me the power of relaxation. I have had the pleasure to interact with many talented individuals and championship coaches. I have discussed the power of relaxation with the late Hall of Fame football coach, George Allen, who never had a losing season as a head coach for twelve years in the NFL; the late performing artist, singer/songwriter John Denver; the Metropolitan Opera House tenor Tony Stevenson; the Japanese Sumo champion Kurosagawa; as well as collegiate national champions, martial art world champions, and professional athletes. With all these people in all these different settings, I witnessed again and again the Art of Relaxation's essential link to peak performance. It is no different when trying to get everyone to perform to the best of their ability when it counts most; namely, in the midst of your company's change initiative.

In every case, regardless of the conditions surrounding your change, your people will perform to the peak of their ability if they are driven from a collective inner strength brought on by clarity of purpose, focus of requirements, and visibility of progress. Before any change can take place, it is your job to set them up to relax and win every day.

5

The Art of Conscious Action

When employees are properly prepared (the Art of Preparation) and meaningfully involved (the Art of Compassion) in the change process, leaders of change can create the conditions for employees to be internally motivated (the Art of Responsibility) and poised for success (the Art of Relaxation). All of this serves as a stage for the fifth Art of Conscious Action. When an organization embraces conscious action, it is able to consistently execute plans and goals because employees embrace company objectives as their own.

Practicing the Art of Conscious Action means that the leaders of change are deeply aware of the need to combine the first four Arts in order to assist everyone in the organization to execute the business plan every single business day. If people are spiritually prepared (Art One), emotionally engaged (Art Two), personally accountable (Art Three), and strategically relaxed (Art Four), then they can act, behave, and deliver results because everyone is consciously aware of the real needs of each other and the business. In other words, execution consistently occurs because the collective spirit of the organization has already embraced the need for and path to change.

The Power of the Moment

I first became familiar with the concept of Conscious Action from my father, the son of a Pennsylvania steel mill foreman who grew up during the Depression. My dad put a high priority on hard work . . . like a marine drill sergeant! "Work before play," he would often say. Or, "Act with a sense of urgency." His famous maxims to me growing up were "money does not grow on trees" and "you may get hit by a bus tomorrow." I never quite pieced it together back then, but I now know the common theme was to appreciate the time and opportunity that each day brings, because tomorrow may never come.

Later in life I learned to create my own maxims for my own family's consumption. My version of "you may get hit by a bus tomorrow" (which always seemed a bit too negative for me) is "this may not be a rehearsal." When people ask me how I have managed to accomplish so much in so many different fields, I usually respond, "Well . . . this life may not be a rehearsal."

I learned long ago that life is precious because we cannot repeat each day. Each moment is the only opportunity you have to be truly grateful, truly positive, and truly significant. To remain on a path where others dictate your actions is to remain disconnected from your spirit. If the people of your organization are to remain fully engaged, they must remain connected to their deepest selves. In short, their daily actions must be consciously meaningful to both the business initiative as well as to them personally.

Step-by-Step, Moment-by-Moment

My experience is that the Art of Conscious Action begins for most people by practicing small steps. Business culture is often so caught up in the big picture, the huge deal, and the major step forward that people overlook the small things they can be doing every moment that will ultimately make a bigger difference in the long run. When you shift to thinking small—moment by moment—you begin to experience the real lasting power of conscious action.

We have all encountered people who declare they have had a life-changing experience. However, without conscious action to follow through, the so-called transformation proves to be only temporary. The same will be true of your company-wide transformation unless you teach your people to act consciously each day over the long haul.

I first experienced the power of conscious action when I chose to not go through seventh-grade confirmation class at my family's Methodist church. This tradition was one where, at the conclusion of the summer study, you officially became an adult member of the church. Even as a seventh grader, I understood that my so-called choice to join the church was not actually mine—it was only the path I was expected to take. I knew in my spirit that I was just a big kid who was not yet qualified to be an official "adult" member of the church. And I also knew that I had no other choices to compare with the choice to go through the confirmation class. I asked my mother, "What if I want to be a Hindu, a

Buddhist, or Jewish, or practice Islam, or whatever?" Joining the church was not a "real" choice until I learned about other educated possibilities. To my amazement, my mother bought my argument as a sincere wish. Instead of forcing me to go to Methodist summer confirmation school, and instead of thinking I was just trying to opt out (albeit creatively) of summertime religious study, she agreed to conduct "home" summer study under her guidance. During that summer, we studied the major religions of the world. So, I guess I am the product of a disciplined drill sergeant (my father) and a theologian (my mother).

This one small step of conscious action (i.e., a summer study of religion) made such an impression that I began to make it a daily habit, looking for significant, conscious choices in my everyday life.

For example, this "habit" of making small conscious actions led me to complete my first year of college, travel, and compete in collegiate downhill ski racing, before many of my peers finished high school. In fact, out of a graduating class of more than 1,000 students, only two of us left high school early with enough advanced credits to head off to college. An interesting point: the girl who joined me in this conscious action was the niece of astronaut Neil Armstrong. We were between our freshman and sophomore year of high school when on July 20, 1969, Armstrong uttered his famous phrase, "That's one small step for a man, one giant leap for mankind." Perhaps it was no coincidence I was linked to this most famous small step.

A Culture of Small, Conscious Choices

Since all big endeavors are made up of a series of small steps, each employee has an opportunity to make many conscious, small decisions throughout each business day. Your job as the change leader is to make sure these conscious decisions remain directed toward the new initiative. It is critical for your people to see the light at this point in your change journey and announce that they are fully on board and focused. But even major "announced" buy-in will not keep your people on board and focused on the right small actions every day.

We all know people who see a bright light and still succumb to their old habits, temptations, and attachments. It is difficult to sustain behavioral change no matter how big the Aha! moment was. This is all to say that it is not enough for your organization to only employ the first four Arts. While they set the stage for successful, sustainable change, you must also learn to practice the new, small actions that will ensure measurable change occurs as planned.

To do so, the senior leadership team must keep the clarity of purpose, focus of requirements, and visibility of progress in front of the organization every business day. Leaders must be unrelenting in this effort because the organization's collective mind will always seek inputs of one kind or another. If the leaders of change are not mindful of this fact, they will falsely assume that one major flash of clarity, focus, and visibility will do the trick. It's just not so.

The fact is that people always need reinforcement. Often,

in more overtly spiritual communities like a church, temple, or synagogue, leaders will continue to mentor and coach (often for a year or more) people desiring to change their behavior. They go on retreats together, continue meeting together regularly, and initiate them into small groups to ensure they remain surrounded by a supportive community. Alcoholics Anonymous is famous for this constant reinforcement of behavioral change.

The Art of Conscious Action is about creating a business-focused reinforcement strategy that plays out on a daily basis. Leaders of change will occupy the collective mind—the consciousness—of the organization at all times so that everyone's actions remain aligned with the desired new direction. This requires a lot of energy and effort. But without this sustained internal marketing campaign, people will see the same old messages coming from senior leadership on high. Without maintaining focus on the change, employees will think the initiative is merely the flavor of the month. A new focus can be achieved in countless innovative ways, but I will highlight a few examples of successful strategies from my experience.

KEEPING THE CHANGE AT THE TOP OF EVERYONE'S MIND

It is possible to establish mechanisms for all functions and all employees to remain clear and focused so that their daily actions at work become conscious actions. These are the conscious actions you are looking for:

1. *Stay on strategy.*

2. *Be consistent with the target behaviors that cure the ills of the business culture.*

3. *Remain directed to those tasks that enable the execution of your new objectives.*

Keeping the successful execution of new objectives visible for all to see—the proof the new behaviors work—is an important way to maintain momentum and focus and occupy the collective mind of the organization. When someone delivers a new objective, it means that he or she is fulfilling exactly what the business needs. When people see the positive results of this, momentum is increased and the initial revelatory buy-in (e.g., "this sounds good") begins to transition into belief (e.g., "this really works"). As the leader, you must work to sustain the momentum of this transition. What follows are three simple measures you can take that have proven to be highly effective.

1. The leader walks the talk = Ongoing clarity of purpose

A first and most important measure is for the president or CEO to personally walk the talk in a highly visible and ongoing basis. This often means completely recalibrating day-to-day responsibilities, delegating operational activities, and thus becoming a living, breathing example of a changed person. There is nothing that better clarifies the purpose of an initiative than the embodiment of new conscious actions in the leader of change.

If the leader of change has a reputation for being closed or autocratic, when he or she starts practicing the Seven Arts for all to see and begins to change, it gives a tremendous boost to the change process. The key, as with personal spiritual development, is that the visible changes must be sincere. You can't fake behavioral change. Over time, people see through insincerity, but they truly respect senior leaders who are willing to say publicly (i.e., visibly) things like "I did not have all the answers before," "I was not leading effectively," or "I was contributing to our organizational distress and poor performance." And then follow up with consistent, new-and-improved actions.

2. Daily fifteen-minute "alignment" meetings = Ongoing focus of requirements

The collective changed behavior you desire often does not occur with consistency unless you frequently show people the core metrics being used to measure improvements. I've found that daily fifteen-minute reminders go a long way to achieving consistent alignment between initial buy-in and ongoing delivery. People need to see on a regular basis that what was proposed to help is actually helping.

With past manufacturing clients, for example, conscious target behaviors are typically those focused on improvement in safety, quality, and productivity. Usually, I suggest that the daily fifteen-minute meetings occur prior to each shift in order for the entire workforce to be aligned on an ongoing basis. The time is highly focused upon the facility's key deliverables against the

operating plan. While safety, quality, and productivity are usually the three key measures to track in manufacturing operations,
this daily fifteen-minute meeting time must also be spent edu-
cating people about the overall direction of the business. This
means "board room awareness" for the entire workforce.

As a template for daily fifteen-minute manufacturing meetings, I usually recommend that the first five minutes be spent
on safety. This visibly demonstrates that the change process is
all about integrity and putting people first. There is no reason
why people should not leave the plant with the same fingers,
toes, and general wholeness as when they walked in the door.
Safety tracking mechanisms should be proactive (recording
"near misses") and not merely reactive. That is to say, keeping
the collective mind proactively focused on safety is far more
effective than learning lessons about safety from an incident
report describing an accident that already occured.

The second five minutes of the daily fifteen-minute manufacturing meeting is recommended to focus on quality. Doing so
accomplishes three important things in a very simple manner.
First, keeping high quality as your prominent manufacturing
objective helps customer focus to remain at the top of the collective mind. Second, high-quality production is the best meas-
urement to capture all the operational benefits you gain when
you make it right the first time. You reduce waste, reduce operating cost, and improve efficiency. Third, the focus on quality
emphasizes that your customers do not really care about all of
your internal operational initiatives. Customers care about the

quality of the products they buy. Asking customers to visit plants where employees are visibly focused on the quality of the customers' purchased products can serve as a big plus to your organization.

I usually recommend that the last five minutes of the daily fifteen-minute meeting be focused on boardroom awareness. Remember: because the culture of your company is in the collective mind of the people, knowledge is key. Raising the level of employee knowledge about competitors, margins, pricing, new customers, industry trends, and executive and/or board decisions is an important step to help every employee remain focused on the right conscious action. When employees truly understand the big picture, it is much easier for them to stay motivated to take the right small steps that will help the company succeed.

In order to do this effectively, facilitators of daily pre-shift meetings need to be trained and developed. These people should have high energy and possess strong interpersonal skills, a good sense of humor, and a propensity to prepare well to motivate and educate teammates to maintain focus and sustain positive momentum.

3. Weekly teleconference or videoconference "state of the union" meetings = Ongoing visibility of progress

This measure provides boardroom awareness on the largest scale. Certainly, the people leading the daily fifteen-minute alignment meetings cannot educate their people on everything that is happening in the company in the final five minutes.

They must focus on giving their people boardroom awareness on a smaller scale—that is, boardroom awareness that applies directly to their day-to-day activities. For the full "state of the union," I encourage companies to initiate weekly meetings that are larger scale in that they involve entire departments, regions, or, at times, entire companies.

The key is for senior leaders to facilitate these meetings following principles consistent with the Seven Arts. Specifically, every meeting should promote (1) participation with open and honest communication by all parties, (2) education, motivation, and empowerment for all participants to execute against plan, and (3) individual responsibility as opposed to an external accountability.

* * *

Over time these weekly meetings become very efficient (they last only twenty to thirty minutes) because all participants in the meeting are trained to come well prepared. As an effective leader of change, how you run meetings in accordance with the Seven Arts is critical. Because operations employees and first line supervisors are primarily the ones leading the daily fifteen-minute meetings, the weekly meetings (video or teleconference) are your prime opportunity to keep yourself and the change message visible for middle- and senior-level managers. In combination, the entire organization can be aligned on a regular basis with constant reminders of conscious actions that promote positive change.

Big Meetings That Motivate
Small, Conscious Actions

Over the years I have seen every kind of meeting, from highly effective to absolutely terrible. In fact, you can sense the collective clarity of purpose, focus of requirements, and visibility of progress in a company simply by attending meetings. Unfortunately, meetings have a bad rap. There have been so many poorly run, poorly motivated meetings throughout most companies' histories that most people walk into meeting rooms with apathy and cynicism oozing from their pores. Therefore, establishing and running focused, relevant, empowering meetings where everyone leaves smarter, clearer, and more focused is a true art. It is also a necessity because meetings are the primary way the leader of change maintains a sense of communal reinforcement throughout the company.

The overarching key is to train yourself and all participants in the discipline of the meeting itself. All attendees should understand how the meeting will run, how it will maintain a focus on the primary objectives, and what questions will be asked of the attendees every time. When significant but tangential problems are noted, the leader needs to have the discipline to reexamine these issues off-line so as not to bog down the planned agenda.

The following parameters will help you ensure participation, education, and promotion of individual responsibility:

1. *The meeting climate must be created such that everyone feels empowered and responsible to speak up in an open and honest*

fashion. For decades, I have used the wisdom of the plant manager, mentioned earlier, and told clients that bad news is good news if it is delivered early. That is, the goal of the meeting is to encourage the discipline of everyone speaking up proactively when they first sense a performance hiccup. The best time to solve problems is to avoid them in the first place, that is, anticipating problems and solving them before they become big problems. If the climate in the meeting is one of intimidation (fear of being blasted), then people will not speak up, and potential problems will remain hidden until it is too late. Your job is to train everyone to think ahead. This can be accomplished by always asking directly if you see any problems that might be developing in the future—this will over time become the expected question and therefore lead to people having answers already in their minds.

2. *The attendees should be trained to start the meeting with their own function-specific report relevant to the measured primary objectives.* They need not waste time reciting the numbers (for example, safety, off-quality, or cost reduction) because the senior leader facilitating the meeting has already seen the data. The real issue is to follow the 80/20 rule; that is, the focus (80 percent) of the reporting and subsequent dialogue should be on the vital few (20 percent) problems that must be addressed early because solving them will have the greatest positive effect on achieving objectives.

Attendees should be prepared to answer the question, "What are the one, two, or three things causing the majority of the data to move in any direction?" Solving for the vital few big contributors of any performance shortfall is key. Everyone who is responsible to give a weekly operations report should eventually be able to anticipate and respond to the question, "What plan of action has already been put in place to correct the shortfall?" This kind of proactive reporting should occur without the senior leader having to ask. This discipline will occur naturally after the first two or three meetings once attendees are educated in the process and told, "This is how I would like the meeting to occur in order to maintain our clarity and focus."

The real reason for the senior leader to be present leading the videoconference or teleconference is to (1) visibly demonstrate concern, (2) offer new information that might shed light on the greater business so that people maintain boardroom awareness, and (3) most importantly, reach into his or her deep pockets (as only the senior leader can) in order to supply added resources (people, capital, technology, etc.) when needed.

The most important question the senior leader should ask is, "Is there anything else you need in order to deliver against your operating plan?"

3. *The collective spirit you aim to create for the meeting is one in which all attendees are holding themselves personally responsible and are thus looking to you to simply help them understand the big picture, secure additional resources if necessary, and leverage*

company-wide practices that you are in a position to offer. If you, as senior leader, are simply acting like the person with the big stick, then you have already removed the collective spirit that is necessary to move the levels of performance to their highest potential.

4. *The efficiency of the meeting lasting only twenty to thirty minutes requires that everyone be present and prepared on time.* People must attend the meeting already prepared to answer standard, routine questions relevant to the primary objectives, and they must have action plans already spelled out. The senior leader should keep a notebook of these meetings and record the deliverables anticipated by the stated and promised corrective action plan.

In other words, the leader of change must record: Who is supposed to do what by when? By recording these promises to deliver, you, as the senior leader of change can refer to your notes and follow up next week in order to demonstrate your ongoing interest, willingness to provide resources, and desire to personally engage the plan and promote clarity and focus.

* * *

Whether we are talking about spiritual development or organizational change management, for an entire enterprise to achieve their highest potential, it is wise to always remember that with right thinking comes right acting. The key for leaders of change in organizations of any size is first to remain personally focused on delivering conscious action that supports the primary objectives; then establish mechanisms that help you reinforce the behavioral changes for all people in all functions every single business day.

And remember, this begins and ends with the right thinking that all positive change happens not by one big Aha! moment but rather by conscious moment-by-moment decisions to act in accordance with the new initiative. This is true whether you are attempting to stop drinking or get into better shape or start climbing to higher levels of organizational effectiveness. In a very poignant and all-encompassing way, I was once reminded of the critical importance the Art of Conscious Action plays in not only our businesses but also our entire lives.

A Conscious and Active Leader

My friend Dr. Akio Urakami was the owner (with his family) of the worldwide Ryobi Motor Products Company, and the president of his company had asked me to be the keynote speaker at their annual North American sales meeting on Hilton Head Island, South Carolina. It was a tremendous privilege. Ryobi makes power tools under the Ryobi brand name, but they have also produced products under the high-profile brand names of Sears Craftsman, Kenmore, and Singer.

By the time I was invited to speak at the annual sales meeting, I had been helping the Ryobi Motor Products Corporation as a management consultant for nearly seven years.

Specifically, I had provided organizational development consulting from the time they bought the Singer Company and transitioned pieces of the company from Japan to South Carolina.

I had also been part of an economic development group helping the state of South Carolina attract overseas companies like Ryobi to locate in the upstate region. For years, working in concert with the State Economic Development Board under the direction of the late Currie Spivey, I assisted the administration of the late South Carolina Governor Carroll Campbell to attract investment and create jobs in South Carolina. This process began with great success under the previous administration led by the Honorable Governor Richard "Dick" W. Riley who later became the United States Secretary of Education, serving for two full terms as a member of President Clinton's cabinet.

Secretary Riley is also one who was instrumental in helping me to establish my consulting business in the 1980s. Through his support and efforts, I began to give brown-bag seminars in Greenville, South Carolina, sponsored by his law firm, Nelson, Mullins, Riley. My first clients were companies attending those seminars endorsed by Governor Riley who was just ending his second term in office.

Many years later as I prepared for my Ryobi speech on the Art of Conscious Action, I was reminded that the opportunity to speak was ultimately created by the daily conscious actions of change leaders like Master Tohei, Currie Spivey, Dr. Urakami, Governor Carroll Campbell, and, in that particular moment, Secretary Dick Riley.

From his initiation and ongoing support of my consulting practice to his ongoing clarity, focus, and visible alignment in helping grow both Furman University (his *alma mater* where I was then a young professor) and the great state of South Carolina, he had truly been (and still is) the conscious leader of positive change I espouse in this chapter.

As I thought about what I would say to my audience, I was grateful to have been given such a tangible experience with the Art I was about to share with them. And there was yet another tangible experience of conscious leadership from which I would draw before I took the stage.

* * *

The sales meeting was a major production. Senior buyers from Home Depot, one of Ryobi's largest and fastest-growing trade customers, would also be present for the three-day national sales meeting extravaganza. A special marketing, media, and promotions company had been hired to ensure the production would run flawlessly. Because I was the keynote speaker, I was asked to be present one full day in advance of my speech. Then I could rehearse the proper cue for my stage entrance complete with strobe lights, special effects, music, hidden microphones . . . the works.

The hype was not my cup of tea, but I had prepared a sincere and hopefully inspiring message that was ultimately about an Art of Conscious Action strategy for maintaining positive sales growth to ensure Ryobi jobs would remain in South Carolina. I also wanted to ensure that our very positive transformation of Ryobi's business systems could be leveraged for added expansion and thus create even more Ryobi jobs and supplier-based manu-facturing jobs. All of this seemed within reach. I was personally invested in this multinational venture being successful from the time I worked in concert with our state government and Dr. Urakami to transition his company stateside.

My investment was not of a monetary nature. It was an investment of conscious action that had been first modeled and then supported by leaders who believed in me and most recently by all the new South Carolina Ryobi employees. These fellow South Carolinians had been asked to turn their factories upside down and make new products using new technology and new processes. The next big step was to take our vision of growth to the wider sales force so that they could understand more deeply that this was a human story of opportunity, change, and growth. My speech would not be "go deliver the sales numbers and get your bonus" hype. A lot more than numbers were at stake, and I knew that what was needed was collective conscious action throughout the sales force.

The rehearsals the day before the big event went well. I was to be (1) on cue at exactly 10:05 a.m., (2) standing on my mark backstage, (3) have my hidden microphones and backup microphones checked and double-checked one last time, and (4) be personally escorted on stage at 10:11 a.m. by the hired pro-duction director. I did not want to throw the timing off, so I was there twenty minutes early.

As I arrived backstage of the hotel's Grand Ballroom, I was handed an urgent message: an emergency call from my mother. My mother? I thought. How does she even know where I am? I learned later that she had contacted my best friend back home who tracked me down. It had taken them more than twenty-four hours.

I ran to the elevators and down the hall to my room where my wife was waiting for me. Tears filled her eyes. She handed me the phone.

"David," my mother said. "Are you there? Are you sitting down?"

I sat on the bed.

"David," she continued after a deep breath, "your father has died."

Tears are welling up now as I write this, just as they ran down my face then. It was 9:55 a.m., eleven minutes from showtime and an elevator ride away from entering a stage with synchronized music and strobe lights. I asked my mother what had happened. My father had gone into the doctor's office for a regular checkup the day before. During a routine throat exam, my father gagged, experienced a sudden heart attack, and died a few hours later in the hospital. My dad had been hit by that bus he'd always told me about.

I honestly never questioned what I had to do in that moment. It is difficult to explain, but I knew that my father— my first consciously active leader—would want me to give the best speech I'd ever given, one great conscious act of leadership and service in his memory.

And I did.

During the speech, I felt as though I was being lifted, guided, and inspired from outside myself. I talked about the commitment of leaders; I spoke about South Carolina jobs and the international economy; I spoke of the conscious action of two South Carolina governors and the presidents of Ryobi, Sears, and Home Depot; I spoke about their personal lives and families and the opportunity to serve and make a difference; and yes, I spoke of my father's many conscious actions and dedicated the speech to his memory. There wasn't a dry eye in the ballroom.

At the close of my speech, I said, "You know, money and jobs do not grow on trees. You have to work hard, use patience and conscious action to meet your goals, and take every opportunity to serve others. There is a bigger picture here—a picture of a larger community of public servants and business leaders who can make a significant difference through your work. That can begin now, today, with small, moment-by-moment decisions to do what is best for the greater good. All this is vitally important. And, do you know why? Because this thing called your life may not be a rehearsal, and you might get hit by a bus tomorrow."

I walked offstage, pointed to heaven, and felt a deep and powerful connection to my father. He was the first to teach me the immense value of embracing conscious action every day. I am ever grateful.

Exceeding Your Own Expectations

Over the past three decades, I've enjoyed the honor of helping organizations large and small, musicians, athletes, and everyday people take their performance to higher and higher levels. And no matter what spiritual and philosophical themes I teach them, in the end it comes down to conscious action. The theme for the Ryobi national sales meeting was "Exceed Your Expectations," and that's what conscious action allows you to do as an individual and an organization of individuals.

The Art of Conscious Action is about aligning your organization with the same clear and focused actions, and then utilizing the visible progress of this alignment to fuel future action and sustain momentum. This approach presumes everyone performs better when they have the right understanding, right knowledge, and right resources to deliver the right results.

For many years, I have seen people astonish themselves with what is truly possible when they act consciously. It is as if executives, managers, and employees suddenly snap out of their low-performance trance and became fully engaged. When this happens throughout an organization, it is nothing short of a spiritual awakening, revealing for the first time what is truly possible when a body of people pledge to grow and develop together for the betterment of the whole.

In this same spirit of growth and peak performance, it is wise to remember the fitting words of leadership expert John Maxwell: "If you do things the way you've always done them, you'll never get more than what you've already gotten."* To perform better, you have to change for the better. To change for the better, you have to act consciously in a better direction.

---

* Max DePree, *Leadership Is an Art*, Dell Publishing, New York, 1989, p. 100.

· 6 ·

THE ART OF WORKING NATURALLY

THE UNIVERSE IS IN FLUX AND EVER CHANGING. To attempt to secure a permanent state of anything—happiness, success, serenity—goes against the very nature of the environment you live in. When you operate from excessive attachment to anything, you actually invite disharmony, isolation, and separation from both people and the reality surrounding you. As a result, your energy weakens, you increasingly struggle to maintain sameness, and eventually you become ill and ungrateful toward those things around you that are constantly changing because they keep you from your utopia.

In the end, total control is a myth because there is so much you cannot and will not ever control. The real power is found in learning to positively control what you can and then adapting to all that you can't control and transforming it into opportunity.

The Japanese call this *reiseishin,* or "universal mind." I call it the Art of Working Naturally. At its core, it is an organization's ability to change what should and can be changed through Arts One through Five, while simultaneously adapting to conditions they cannot control. On an individual level, it means simultaneously living out of self-control and self-sacrifice.

CONNECTED

I was once honored to have a personal audience with the Emperor of Japan, His Majesty Emperor Akihito. I had received the Crown Prince Akihito Foundation Award, which is given each year to a person, or persons, who are scholars of some aspect of Japanese culture and are often also proficient practitioners of a uniquely Japanese art or discipline. In my case, the award was related to my study, development, and practice of *Ki-Aikido* under Master Tohei.

I was escorted by three limousines bearing the flags of Japan and the United States from the Keidanren government office building to the Akasaka Palace. Upon arriving at the palace, I was taken through the personal living quarters of the royal family and into a special meeting room for guests. The room was specifically designed to help foster intimate conversation and connection. I learned that this connection was to be between not only His Majesty and his guests (the inside world) but also between his guests and nature (the outside world).

As we approached the special meeting room, the door was opened by an Imperial Household attendant. Standing before me was His Majesty dressed in a gray suit made of shiny silk. Immediately, I bowed respectfully and deeply. Unbeknownst to me (because my head was lowered), at the exact same time His Majesty extended his right hand for a proper Western-style handshake. A staff photographer was already positioned inside the room prepared to capture the very first moment of our formal introduction. The humorous photograph he captured was of His Majesty standing elegantly in an upright posture extending his pointed right hand to the tip of my bowed head.

After we corrected the awkward but funny situation with many out-of-sync bows and miss-cued handshakes, the Keidanren staff and Imperial Household attendants departed. Only His Majesty and His Majesty's personal aide, Grand Chamberlain Watanabe, and two other recipients remained. They were pleased to let me look around and get caught up in admiration of the room.

One entire wall, floor to ceiling, was a giant glass aquarium housing rare species of primitive-looking fish (His Majesty's father, Emperor Hirohito, had been a highly trained ichthyologist). The entire wall opposite the aquarium was also floor-to-ceiling glass that revealed the spectacular outdoors and specifically, the private garden of the royal family. It was the most beautiful, manicured garden I had ever seen. The rest of the room was otherwise empty. Two *ikebana* (floral arrangements) sat on small tables near the two other opposing walls, and the only other furniture in the room was a small sitting couch for His Majesty's guests, two sitting chairs, one for His Majesty and one for the Grand Chamberlain, and a small coffee table between us with beautiful pastries crafted in the shape of exotic birds. If there was ever an environment to connect individuals with each other and nature simultaneously, this room was the place.

At the time of the meeting, I was conducting research on environmental ethics, and so I started the conversation by simply admiring the setting. I described to His Majesty the splendor of the room, the feeling of intimacy, and the connection to nature and each other. He smiled knowingly and immediately shared his interest in environmental protection.

We struck up an enlightening conversation about the social/moral/political concept of rights as entitlements. In the Western philosophical tradition, human beings are deemed to have inalienable rights, for example, "life, liberty, and the pursuit of happiness." I asked His Majesty if he believed the concept of rights as an inalienable entitlement could be extended to include non-human entities—animals, plants, and so on—and if so, might this serve as a basis for environmental protection?

His Majesty's response was wonderful. While he explained that the Japanese tradition espoused a nature-centered (ecocentric) worldview, as opposed to a human-centered (homocentric or egocentric) or a God-centered (theocentric) worldview, His Majesty added that he did not believe you could simply extend to nature, to the external world, or to anything non-human, the Western notion of human rights.

"It is not as simple," he continued, "as thinking one man is deserving of moral entitlements and so does this precious tree [pointing outside] or this rare species of fish [pointing to the aquarium]." Then His Majesty paused and, pointing to the two of us, said, "We, on the other hand, have an obligation to cultivate within us a connection, a relationship of between-ness, so that we can feel that we are all in this universe together."

They were memorable words that echoed the teaching of Master Tohei who ultimately taught me what it means to embrace and enact the Art of Working Naturally in an organization.

THE NATURE OF SUSTAINED SUCCESS

It is unnatural to attempt to sustain success without becoming more and more connected to not only those inside your organization but also those outside it. Said another way, it is natural (and consequentially more sustainable) for an organization to connect and positively change what it can on the inside (Arts One through Five) while simultaneously ensuring it connects with and positively changes those on the outside—customers, communities, and, yes, even other companies. The more connected an organization is—inside and out—the stronger and more sustainable it is. His Majesty Emperor Akihito understood this well. When a connection on both the inside and the outside occurs, all that flows from those relationships is stronger and more sustainable because it is our nature to be connected. This was the reason His Majesty's meeting room was set up in the manner it was. He was promoting an inner connection (between him and his guests) and, at the same time, an outer connection (between us and the natural world itself).

When your people become more deeply connected—spiritually connected—inside your walls through Arts One through Four, they are set up to individually succeed in the change initiative through clear, focused, and visible action (Art Five). The application of these first five Arts will thus allow your company to understand, embrace, and initiate the change. Your next progression is twofold:

1. *Ensure the current change initiative is sustained all the way through.*

2. *Prepare your organization for all future changes . . . because they will come.*

These are the results of applying the sixth Art of Working Naturally. It banks on the closely related concepts of unity and reciprocity.

When your organization is spiritually connected inside its walls, it is strengthened through unity and ongoing give and take. People who are well connected are able to make personal sacrifices for each other and the company's greater good. There is simultaneous self-control and self-sacrifice. Execution occurs consistently and successfully.

Those who continue to act as autocratic managers, holding on to their own personal agendas, must be counseled further. These openly determined resisters or passive resisters are quickly provided with more leader development assistance. It is sad that such persons know no school of leadership other than the School of the Use of the Big Stick. If additional leader training does not help, the manager is asked to excel at another organization where, sadly, verbal abuse seems to be the accepted norm in the name of "it's just business." This is the best possible way to sustain the spirit of an organization growing and developing in a positive direction.

Yet, an organization is only a small world in the midst of the much larger world of business and, beyond that, the whole of the world itself. The Art of Working Naturally is also about using the newfound spiritual strength and proficiency within your company walls to connect with and improve the greater good of the world itself.

When your spiritually connected organization reaches beyond its walls to extend Arts One through Five with people and entities outside its walls, it is strengthened by a greater number of advocates. It is also able to quickly and properly adapt to changes beyond its control as its ears, eyes, and hands are multiplied. When such characteristics are true of an organization, it is possible for it to remain in business for decades—even a century or more. Getting there is truly an Art.

Making Natural Connections Outside Your Walls

As all experienced executives know, there is nothing more frustrating than a business partnership where one company represents itself with multiple faces. Companies that partner well with other companies for mutual gain do so by virtue of their ability to focus and communicate effectively and consistently, presenting an aligned single face to the partner company. Once your company is properly aligned against the new strategic plan, it is possible to extend the benefits of the highly disciplined, high-performance culture by inviting other companies into your tent of accelerated performance improvement.

The Art of Working Naturally is thus the practice of naturally extending your company's alignment to include other companies for mutual gain. Again, this is natural because we humans are already fundamentally connected. Any time you can create a win/win, you have elevated a natural connection to one that produces more value, growth, and development opportunities for everyone involved.

To begin the process, the senior leadership of your business must first understand the enormous advantages and potential benefits of partnering effectively with the external world in which you already intersect. The truism to keep in mind is that all businesses survive only if there is some form of value creation that someone is willing to pay for. At the end of the day, business is about value creation. The Art of Working Naturally means putting into practice those activities that enable you to sustain value creation both inside and outside your walls.

You've already done the natural connecting work inside your walls through Arts One through Five, so your primary role now is to connect more significantly and strategically with your customers, suppliers, and research and development collaborators.

This is accomplished by re-employing the first five Arts to the key relationships outside your walls. In this way you naturally extend the benefits of your internal change initiative to your full asset base.

You will prepare for, assess, and articulate how the new partnership process (or extended change initiative) will be conveyed and managed (Arts One through Three). You will then establish timetables for deliverables and the tangible objectives to be developed, managed, and measured (Arts Four and Five).

Moving away from a transactional relationship and toward a partnership like this requires considerable alignment and uncharacteristic understanding. Yet, when these are accomplished across your organization's entire value chain, it can take all parties involved to the highest level of performance.

The business case for optimizing the full asset base is undeniable. Every business is both a customer and a supplier, and when you view the entire enterprise end to end in this manner, it is only natural to unlock the full potential of all the people involved by preparing, developing, and connecting them at the strongest, most sustainable level: their spirits.

This greater collective mindset is in direct opposition to the typical corporate mindset that focuses on protecting its own interests, demanding price concessions, and other disconnected practices that often become self-defeating over the long haul.

The average consumer products business spends between one third and one half of revenues on direct materials with strategic suppliers. This large expense should alone prove the need for senior leadership to give as much attention to strategic spiritual connection outside company walls as they do for the core business.

But where exactly should your attention be focused? Should every outsider be initiated into the Seven Arts process? Let's answer that.

The Who and How of Extending Your Reach

Not all customers and suppliers represent a "strategic" interdependency. Establishing the correct selection criteria is key. In my experience, the practice of extending the Seven Arts between two or more partner companies first requires some basic directional likenesses. I say "directional" because at the beginning of the strategic partnership, the cultures of both companies are clearly not yet integrated, aligned, and focused. Therefore, the top-to-top relationship between the senior leaders must first express a desire "directionally" to see the partnership in a strategic manner. Once that has been confirmed, then the selection criteria for strategic partnership can begin by considering four basic questions related to your own company's needs.

1. *Where does your company want to go?*

2. *Where are you now?*

3. *How will you prioritize your potential partner's plans and then set joint criteria for choosing additional partners?*

4. *How will you get it done together?*

The first question, "Where does your company want to go?" assumes that your company is already aligned and focused internally and already achieving measurable performance improvement. Now you wish to extend the benefits across the whole of the enterprise. Since the time and energy needed to create a successful partnership is significant, you want to first analyze the financial returns that would result if the strategic partnership was executed successfully. Such a proactive economic analysis is as simple as quantifying the investment and return on investment of organizational time and resources that executing a strategic partnership will require.

Answering the second question, "Where are you now?" requires gathering strategic information. This process must take a pragmatic, realistic approach by critically examining your company's internal competencies. For example, you must ask, "What are the internal strengths and weaknesses of my key customer accounts, my sales team, and my competitive research?" Or, "How likely is it that my company will secure big wins in the competitive marketplace?" Once your true strengths, weaknesses, and gaps are honestly and accurately identified, you can conduct a similar analysis of your potential partners.

This kind of early analysis is required to match joint economic payback with real internal needs and real external capabilities that can fulfill the needs if properly executed. This analysis also allows you and your partners to prioritize the degree of difficulty in the joint endeavor.

The third question is, "How will you prioritize your

partner's development plans and then set joint criteria for choosing additional outside partners?" In addition to working backward to determine the joint economic payback, you must also consider future cultural issues and future partner relationship issues that may affect things like product exclusivity or patent ownership or access to proprietary technology used in the joint effort. Companies outside your current realm of influence that generally make poor future partners are those with a collective mindset that

- Prefers a market-transaction or buy-sell dynamic
- Only thinks about the short term
- Has a misaligned and unfocused collective spirit
- Lacks vision from their senior leadership
- Works poorly in a matrix management environment
- Diverts responsibility for poor quality or late delivery
- Shows little flexibility in their contracts, based upon a lack of trust

In contrast, companies that would become an immediate candidate for an additional strategic partnership are those that

- Evidence a willingness to adopt the Seven Arts change process
- Exhibit long-term strategic thinking

- Have visionaries in their leadership
- Are open with information
- Espouse a continuous improvement philosophy for people and processes
- Are receptive to new thinking
- Welcome risk taking
- Are comfortable with matrix management
- Encourage high levels of trust with partner companies
- Have learned to manage confidentiality well (no leaks)
- Readily accept responsibility for problems and quickly focus on root-cause analysis and immediate resolution

The fourth question, "How will you get it done together?" is where your experience practicing the first five Arts in your organization (particularly the Art of Relaxation and Art of Conscious Action) is your greatest asset.

At the end of the day, executing the strategic partnership requires organizational development and change management expertise that is already a proven internal competency of your company. Initially, you can assign change leaders to the strategic partnership who have already experienced success creating spiritual alignment and clear and measurable focus in your own company.

Tactically speaking, partner companies will always need to co-develop the high-profile metrics for the primary partnership activities (Art of Relaxation), just as you developed clear metrics to drive significant improvement in your own company. You will also need to share detailed, project-specific development plans in order to track progress on an ongoing basis. Roles and responsibilities for executing X, Y, and Z, must then remain clear, focused, and visible (Art of Conscious Action). Conflict resolution plans should be discussed at the onset since some problems will inevitably occur along the way (Art of Compassion). Top-to-top CEO and senior leadership briefings should occur every quarter, and then, virtually all of the established mechanisms for each of the first five Arts should be appropriately replicated in order to ensure deep connectedness (Art of Preparation) between both companies that engenders daily compassion (Art of Compassion), personal accountability (Art of Responsibility), and relaxed and focused action (Art of Relaxation and Art of Conscious Action).

Extending the benefits of improved revenue generation and cost reduction in this way will ultimately create a stronger, more viable company capable of growing in the most competitive business environment or most difficult economic conditions. The overarching key to initiating the Art of Working Naturally is acknowledging that you cannot reach peak effectiveness alone—as an individual or as an organization. Once you've initiated successful, spiritually based change within your organization, the most natural (and most strategic) thing you can do is reach outside your walls and extend the positive results to every other individual and entity within your reach.

When you learn to apply the Art of Working Naturally, you are then ready to embrace the last of the Seven Arts. It is the one Art that brings all the other Arts into proper perspective and highest significance.

THE ART OF SERVICE

I'M BETTING THE ART OF SERVICE is not quite what you are thinking. While serving others, and thus the greater good, is the overall goal of this Art, the means by which your organization practices it is not simply a matter of serving others across the value chain. It is much more.

Ultimately, the Art of Service is about openness, flexibility, and detachment from the outcomes you desire. These qualities allow you to be in a place of service every minute of every day, especially in the face of challenges and adversity. This does not mean you stop progressing in the direction you believe is right. Nor does it mean you stop caring whether you succeed or fail. It means you stay prepared for the obstacles that will always arise.

Remaining open, flexible, and detached to specific outcomes allows your organization to keep its collective mind (its spirit) open to new paths for success and greater opportunities for partnering, collaboration, and greater-good thinking, even in the midst of obstacles.

In the practice of *Ki-Aikido*, it is this free and flexible state that enables you to utilize your attacker's forceful strike to disarm him. If you are not prepared in this way, you will either meet his strike with resistance or miss the opportunity to "serve" him by disarming him without injuring him.

In organization speak, this attacker's strike might symbolize a competitor making a swift move to gain the upper hand. It may also symbolize pummeling economic conditions that would cause a typical organization to become tense, defensive, and myopic in their thoughts and actions. In such a state, an organization misses the opportunities to serve the greater good all around them—the opportunities that will ultimately keep them in the game.

Let me explain this in greater detail by telling you about an experience I once had while teaching the Art of Service to an unreceptive audience (at least not initially).

How to Take a Body Check

One year I was demonstrating this very point at a sports psychology conference in Miami, Florida. I was a speaker along with many others including Hall of Fame NFL coach George Allen. The theme was peak performance, and on the first day, I gave a presentation to a group of about fifty people, many of whom were active players and coaches in the NHL.

At the end of the session, I was illustrating how it is possible to not receive an opposing hockey player's body check by maintaining this free and fully aware state of service. The problem was that these professional hockey players saw themselves as tough guys and did not take kindly to a smaller philosophy professor telling them how to play hockey. By their body language I could tell they were skeptical throughout my entire talk.

I had performed these *Ki* development demonstrations enough to know when the people in the audience were ready for a tangible challenge. In these situations, audience participation was always helpful.

I calmly knelt in my street clothes and asked five big, strong NHL professional and collegiate hockey players to join me onstage and line up behind one another to push me over. I kept my upper body upright and asked the first big guy who stood opposite me to place his large hands squarely on my shoulders in order to push me backward with all his power. Then the second, third, fourth, and fifth hockey player stood behind the first guy in a train, such that all five tough guys were attempting to push me over using the combined power of their bulging legs, strong backs, and thick arms.

I normally don't like doing these showy kinds of demonstrations. But sometimes in order to truly serve new students who do not yet believe in the power of the Art of Service, I need to grab their attention in some dramatic manner. By actually giving all five of these strong men a simultaneous personal experience of my not receiving their tremendous power, I could gain not only their attention and respect, but also the attention and respect of all the others in the audience.

On my cue the five players began to push, tentatively at first and then in increasing measure as they realized I was not moving. The first player then leaned into the effort at an angle, trying to drive me over backward. The other four followed suit behind him. They were all heaving and grunting.

The more they pushed, the more I allowed their force to pass into my center and dissipate. Master Tohei called this the "Magic Pot." In the end, they couldn't push me over, and I had the captive attention of that audience of fifty for the rest of my talk.

SERVING IN THE TOUGHEST CONDITIONS

When I tell you the rest of the story, you'll understand why I say I might have been better off to leave it at that one demonstration. Unfortunately, the first demonstration worked so well that the hotel guests were buzzing all night about how this little, martial arts, philosopher guy had done this unbelievable demonstration with a bunch of big, strong NHL players. The actual players who I used in the demonstration gave further testimony (at the hotel bar, I assume) telling everyone who would listen how amazing it all was.

Early the next morning, the conference organizers asked if I would do a repeat performance and give a second, expanded session that afternoon. These organizers said they wanted to open the hotel's grand ballroom to accommodate everyone who wanted to attend. I told them, "no problem."

By early afternoon the grand ballroom was packed. Again, it was a tough-guy crowd of about 300 people affiliated with the NHL, NFL, collegiate athletics, and sports psychology presenters. I think one of the very few women in the place was my mother who had accompanied my father to Miami—he was a George Allen fan.

While teaching me the Art of Service, Master Tohei frequently used the phrase "Satisfy the feeling." That is, when someone wants a piece of you, when they want to attack you, destroy you, put you down, then by all means . . . "let them come and satisfy the feeling." Then he would follow it up with "if you like to fall, then come. Otherwise, be nice."

I recalled his clever monologue as I prepared for my encore talk. Given the rumor mill at the hotel, I knew the large crowd was there for one reason only. They wanted to satisfy the feeling—some to see me pushed over successfully, and some to see me successfully dissipate the "attack." So, I decided that rather than giving my presentation on "*Ki* and Peak Performance" first and then provide demonstrations at the end of the session (as I did the day before), this time I would just give them what they wanted right away. I knew that once I conducted the demonstration, I would be able to teach them effectively.

I took the stage and began by asking ten strong men (doubling the number from the previous day) to please join me on stage. There was no hesitation. Ten of the strongest hockey defensemen and football linebackers showed up on stage. I stacked them all in front of me just as I had done the day before and then knelt on both knees with my torso upright.

I then instructed them to begin pushing.

Having either seen or heard about the previous day's demonstration, these ten big men were ready to drive me through the stage, ballroom floor, and concrete beneath that. And I knew about half the audience hoped they would. But just like the day before, as the force of the ten strong men came against me, I simply relaxed completely and purposefully, allowing their power to settle into my center, Master Tohei's "Magic Pot," and remained unmoved.

In this particular demonstration, however, one little problem developed as I was redirecting the massive force. I was wearing my street clothes again, rather than a martial arts uniform, and this was not the best idea. There is a reason martial arts uniforms are loose and stretchy. My cotton pants were not.

About ten seconds into the demonstration, my pants bore the full ten-bodied force. While my body did not move, my pants crotch exploded from the front zipper to my backside belt loop. And I mean the seams burst apart and made a huge popping noise. I was suddenly kneeling in front of a standing-room-only crowd in a grand ballroom at the start of a two-and-a-half-hour presentation with a gapping hole in my crotch.

Immodesty aside, people were still amazed except for one woman in the center aisle who was laughing hysterically—thanks mom. I didn't find as much humor in it as she did but I knew the point had been made in an even more provocative fashion than I had planned. Someone quickly handed me a towel. I wrapped it around my waist locker-room style and continued teaching like this for the rest of my session. I didn't mind, and I knew they didn't either. They had just experienced the incredible and unexpected power of the Art of Service.

Your organization can experience and possess the same power if you learn to stop resisting challenges and adversities.

When everyone in your company does so, you can transform problems or obstacles into opportunities for greater achievement and significance.

ALL DAY, EVERY DAY SERVICE

The key to applying the Art of Service is simply to take all the benefits of the first six Arts and put them into practice daily, especially when you face adversity. You and your people are transforming yourselves every day when you operate from the spiritual strength of your prepared, compassionate, responsible, relaxed, and conscious selves.

Since I always saw Master Tohei teach, I once asked him when he practiced.

"Twenty-four hours a day," he replied.

In other words, his practice for *Ki-Aikido* was in remaining open, flexible, and detached all day long in order to remain available to serve others.

His statement became more tangible to me when the following day, while serving as his *otomo* and riding quietly in the back seat of a car with him, I noticed him moving his head and body ever so slightly while his eyes remained closed. I quietly watched, trying to figure out what he was doing. After a few minutes, I could see by his rhythmic movement that he seemed to be practicing the traditional movements of *Ki-Aikido* in his head.

Accordingly, I somewhat jokingly leaned over to my teacher and softly asked, *"Keiko desu ka?"* ("Are you practicing?"). He responded with a nod. He was always prepared to serve others through the "compassionate art" of *Ki-Aikido*.

This same spirit of twenty-four-hour service is achieved in an organization when its people practice applying the Seven Arts throughout their daily lives, on the job and off it. More prepared, compassionate, responsible, relaxed, conscious, natural, and others-focused efforts will reap benefits twenty-four hours a day, not only in the lives of your people but also in the lives of those they love.

Bringing It Home

In these final pages, I want to change the tone. I'd like to engage you in a heart-to-heart, reflective conversation about your life on the whole. Are you happy? Are you satisfied at work? Is there a compelling reason you go? Do you believe you are growing and developing in valuable, meaningful ways while there? Do you have a positive outlook about the future?

The Art of Service is of course about putting other people's needs first. And this task can be a difficult one when we feel our needs are not being met in the first place. But that is the paradox of service: when we put others' needs first, our needs are met somehow in a more abundant way than if we had spent our entire day—or lives—feeding our needs. This is why all spiritual traditions espouse the basic theme to "love thy neighbor" and "do unto others as you would have them do unto you." Where organizational change is concerned, this simply means serving others in order to best facilitate ongoing and ever-improving change. When you and every other person in your organization are committed to this everyday practice, change is never hindered in any way, and individual and organizational needs are met in abundance.

Reflect now on your deeper sense of purpose and the opportunities for growth and development at work that support this deeper purpose. I'm basically asking you to reflect honestly on your choice to be happy and fulfilled at work or not. I'm asking because you must examine your present condition sincerely and honestly if your aim is to use your work as a vehicle for personal, spiritual growth.

These spiritual questions that I pose are simply intended to encourage you to reflect deeply in this present moment on your legacy during your lifetime of employment.

How will people remember the way you worked and lived with others during your career?

How will co-workers and employees actually remember you? How will they think about you? What about the legacy of your leadership? Your integrity? Did you do what you said? Did you lead by example? Did you make a positive difference in your work life every day?

I am asking you these questions now in the present moment because you may recall that this is the only time that you or anyone else can change. Recommitting yourself to pursuing and following your personal greater good only happens when you reflect deeply and honestly upon your shortcomings. And as I have said, being committed to your greater good is the catalyst for your organization's greater good.

If you are a supervisor, manager, or senior leader in a company who is charged with leading change, then imagine the added gift that your present position affords you and those around you. You are in a position of spiritual leadership. So what exactly are you going to do with this gift, this opportunity for personal, organizational, and, ultimately, global spiritual growth?

ALL SIGNIFICANT ORGANIZATIONAL DEVELOPMENT IS SPIRITUAL

Perhaps it is no coincidence how much spiritual development has in common with organizational development.

First, a person grows spiritually only when he or she internalizes deeply a need to change. In the same way, organizations only change when its individuals understand and personally anchor the need to change.

Second, spiritual development occurs only when you commit yourself deeply to the change process every single day. Positive organizational development occurs only when the "spiritual guides," the leaders of change and those they are leading, are deeply committed to executing the change process every day.

Third, both spiritual development and organizational development can occur only when the mind of the individual or collective mind (i.e., the culture) of the business changes. The mind must change enough such that actual behaviors change for good.

Fourth, both spiritual development and organizational development can get off to a sudden positive start—an "overnight change" experience—in reaction to some kind of significant crisis fueling the sense of urgency. However, sustaining these changes over time represents the real challenge.

Fifth, successful spiritual development and successful organizational development occur only when they are regarded as deeply significant at a personal level. This naturally occurs with spiritual development. It does not naturally occur with business development—but it should. In today's world of outsourcing, continued employment often depends on a business's ability to change dramatically how goods and services are designed, developed, and brought to the global marketplace. This means that an organization's survival depends upon executing successfully new ways of conducting business. Failure to execute change in business can mean the loss of a breadwinner's job. When this happens, families suffer a crushing blow that is deeply personal and significant. Therefore, organizational development success is deeply significant and must be understood by each individual in the organization as such. The change initiative must be understood at a personal level just as a crisis in one's personal life must be internalized in order to prepare a person for lasting change.

Sixth, and most powerfully, most already have experience with both spiritual development and organizational development. Most people have some kind of spiritual life, and most people have to work for a living. In both cases, it is likely that you have already experienced significant change, and so you can reflect upon your own experience and begin to see these six connections between spiritual development and organizational development for yourself. You have likely already experienced change in your spiritual outlook or spiritual commitments due to various events in your personal life. And you have likely experienced change in your work outlook or employment commitments due to various efforts by your company to improve, remain competitive, grow and develop, or maybe just survive in the competitive global business environment.

With all six of the common characteristics between spiritual development and organizational development, I believe it makes sense to view the process of successfully leading change in the workplace as one that is linked to leading spiritual growth to a deeper level. The approach to leading change in business can be as serious and important as leading spiritual development especially when we all consider how much of our lives we spend at work.

Your Greatest Opportunity to Grow

Why shouldn't business growth and development (and sometimes survival) be an occasion to develop ourselves in deep spiritual ways? Why can't our daily experiences at work support our spiritual development when we, in fact, spend so much of our time in work-related relationships? Since serving others is a cornerstone of practicing your spiritual development in daily life, then what better place to practice the Art of Service than at work. Work is where you spend most of your daily life—between one-half and two-thirds of it, in fact—

and so it is where you can best enhance the quality of life and that of others.

Moreover, the Seven Arts of Preparation, Compassion, Responsibility, Relaxation, Conscious Action, Working Naturally, and Service are all consistent with the practice of spiritually developing yourself. Your work life can and should serve as your greatest asset when it comes to focusing on bettering yourself and following your highest good. Your work can be the primary stage and arena in which you craft your highest good in the service of humanity's highest good. Most people miss a tremendous opportunity to view change differently in the workplace.

In all my years of leading change by improving the quality of other people's work life, and thereby, improving the business performance of my client companies, I have always known that I was serving a higher calling. This higher calling to bring about positive change is fueled by a deep desire to actualize my own highest potential in the now (not when my physician tells me, for instance, that I have one month to live).

In this context, I believe it is a shame that so many businesses fail to lead change successfully; they fail to see the challenge as a significant gift and calling for everyone to achieve their highest potential by serving others in the workplace. Instead, the mindset in business is often, "Our backs are up against a wall," or, "We were forced into this hellish situation," or, "We have to change, and it won't be fun."

Companies naively venture into the change process with this negative, empty mindset. And instead of being sensitive to the spiritual opportunity before them, executives mechanically throw a lot of time, money, and resources at consultants and training programs. And nothing significant happens. Or it happens, and then a year later the same need arises again because they company has fallen back into the way it was always done.

All companies realize at some point that they need to streamline operations and cut out waste and inefficiency. Most simply throw money and consultants at the initiative, and yet people still resist applying the new tools, skills, or procedures they have learned because their collective mind has not changed. They see no deep, spiritual significance to the change process, and so they commit on only a surface level.

Unless people are truly engaged in the change process using the Seven Arts, they will not view the culture change initiatives and performance improvement initiatives as a higher calling with deep personal significance for their lives.

IMMERSED IN SERVICE

There is a seventh common denominator between successful spiritual development and successful organizational development that I haven't mentioned. In fact, it applies whether the transformational work is in the area of athletics, music, breaking addictions, spiritual growth, or change management. I call it *immersion*.

Monastic life is meant to create the experience of immersion in the sense of cultivating yourself twenty-four hours a day in support of your genuine desire for spiritual transformation as a human being. In organizations with whom I work, I underscore the importance of making a complete personal commitment, or immersion, in order to change bad or counterproductive habits of thinking and behavior. For this reason, I offer a perspective that encourages you to make your work life your most significant vehicle for deep, spiritual transformation.

We all have the same amount of time to get things done. Those who accomplish important tasks, who are highly productive, who learn from their mistakes, who change for the better . . . are those who alter what is done right now.

So, when you contemplate the amount of time—that is, the amount of present moments—spent in your work life, it makes sense to view the commitment of time as a primary contributor to your overall life legacy. Your life itself is your monastery, and your work takes up most of the rooms inside.

By making your entire day, twenty-four hours a day, a series of present moments for prepared, compassionate, responsible, relaxed, conscious, and natural service, you are immersing yourself in ongoing spiritual development, interpersonal development, and business development every day.

This is a fundamentally different way of thinking and acting in utter contrast with the norm that assumes, "I will be at my best outside of work where I am happier, and I will be miserable at work where the stresses, strains, and pressure to perform get me down."

Down this path, you are missing the joy of living your whole life in a unified, significant manner where all activity points to your higher calling to serve the greater good.

A COMMUNITY OF SERVICE

Let me clarify exactly what I mean by this. In three decades of consulting, I have not sought to merely dress change management in spiritual development clothing. What I have tried to do is explain the level of commitment required to make successful change. I do so by discussing the nature of the deepest, most significant kind of change: spiritual.

This is why I start the change process by sitting down with the primary change leader and asking him or her, "What is your legacy going to be?" I want to know about the leader's whole life and learn what he or she is doing as a person (not just a business person) to reach his/her highest potential.

I need to understand the CEO as a whole person, including what makes him or her tick. If I get negative feedback about the CEO down the road in the difficult change process, then I want to know up front if this CEO is willing and able to lead change by changing themselves first. Without change-related leadership at the top, it is not likely that I, the Seven Arts, or anybody else is going to be successful guiding a positive business transformation with dramatic, measurable performance improvement.

Immersion then, is when the leaders of change view the organization as a spiritual, even monastic, community. The organization does, in fact, live as a community. The people who make up that community are either aligned, committed, and focused or they are not. When they are, they can elevate performance levels often higher than anyone imagined.

In the end, the Seven Arts applied collectively invite individuals into the monastic community. The Art of Service occurs when (1) everyone is immersed in the process willingly, (2) the barriers to performance improvement fall away, (3) obstacles (including negative people) get out of the way, and (4) resistance crumbles. People are smiling, people are happy, people are helping each other, and people see themselves as winners at work.

You can feel when this is occurring. People arrive to work ready and willing. They leave work happy which makes them better family members when they walk through the front door at home. For the typical employee, the best part of the day is no longer seeing the office building in the rearview mirror. There is no longer a massive sigh of emotional relief when the workday is done. And weekday morning dread fades away.

When the Art of Service is added to the previous six Arts, the highest goal becomes for all employees to simultaneously receive and give fulfillment by using work moments to create a community of individuals who serve and are served.

SECURING A SERVICE COMMUNITY

A great example of such a community occurred, of all places, in two Las Vegas casinos. For years, I trained all the security people at Caesar's Palace and the Mirage Casino and Resort Hotels there. In a gambling environment, the security challenge is enormous. Every night, the big casinos are frequented by "bad guys." Some are so bad that they bring their own personal bodyguards. They get high or drunk or both, and then they get hostile because they lose a lot of money.

While this is happening each night, families and friends are strolling through to eat dinner, return to their hotel rooms, or enjoy some good innocent fun. And this sort of fun is what the owners wanted. Much of Las Vegas has been reshaped and reinvented by a few visionary business owners like Steve Wynn over the last two decades in order to transform the area into a suitable destination for families. I was hired to teach the security force at these two popular resorts how to ensure that reputation remained.

The challenge was changing a large security staff from strong-armers to servants. I had taught them to meet unexpected uprisings professionally, politely, and calmly. Their work had to always be tactful and inconspicuous because it was typically performed amidst a crowded casino full of nice people trying to enjoy their vacation. This was achieved practically by training the security staffers in *Ki-Aikido* techniques. The change stuck because I also taught the security officials the deeper message—that their highest calling was to serve all patrons—even the bad guys.

Each day of training consisted of a combination of customer service guidance and arrest control. When we discussed serving the customers of the casinos, I explained the *Ki-Aikido* principle of remaining calm under duress. In this way, the security officers learned to use their mind clearly when facing adversity and potentially violent situations. When I trained them in arrest control techniques, we would clear the furniture from a hotel ballroom and use the room as a large *dojo,* demonstrating everything from how to handle misdemeanor arrests to confrontational felony arrest situations.

Over the course of two and a half years, I witnessed how the work and personal lives of these security professionals were totally transformed when they came to understand the Art of Service. Namely, that their job was not to control, manipulate, or strong-arm the bad guys but rather to serve the greater good of everyone in the entire casino, including the offenders. Once the collective mind of the large security staff embraced the Art of Service, each security officer learned to remain prepared, compassionate, responsible, relaxed, conscious, and natural so that their every action elevated every customer's experience.

With this subtle but significant change to the environment of the two large casinos, families and friends could enjoy themselves with confidence that they were not only protected but also valued. And I'd like to think that in some way, the offenders each night were affected positively as well, not unlike the young father who held the patrons of the Woody Creek Tavern hostage.

The benefits didn't end there.

The security officers—the true leaders of sustained positive change at those casinos—learned to apply the Art of Service at home. The change initiative at work changed each individual on the whole, at the deepest level. In the end, this is what I desire for you and each person in the organization you lead.

SERVICE NOW, WHEREVER YOU ARE

My father was a Rotarian, a little league coach, a school board member, and a dentist (among other things). In all these capacities he was truly a service provider in his everyday life. In my office at home stands a plaque that was given to him in 1968. It reads:

Barrington Public Schools
To Charles H. Shaner
In Grateful Appreciation for Your
Unselfish Interests in the Education
Of the Youth of Barrington

This plaque is priceless to me because it serves as a daily reminder of the importance of the Art of Service. It is both the linchpin and the culmination of the Seven Arts. Your own life is always enriched whenever you can contribute to another's accomplishment.

In the end, the first six Arts teach you how organizational change occurs by transforming individuals at their deepest level. This final Art of Service reminds you that individual transformation is ultimately for the purpose of serving a greater good. We have an obligation, as His Majesty Emperor Akihito said, to each other, as "we are all in this universe together."

It is through service that your transformation journey ends up where it should—with a focus outside yourself, on the needs of others. By practicing all Seven Arts, you move from a selfish mind focused on personal needs to a service mind focused on improving others through your own improvement. When this happens company-wide, any change is possible.

I hope you can now see that organizational change is far more significant than most ever imagine. The universal problem, noted Leo Tolstoy, is that, "Everyone thinks of changing the world, but no one thinks of changing himself."* We might say it this way: Everyone thinks of changing the company, but no one thinks that means changing himself.

I hope, for a change, you will think differently. Change yourself first and you truly can change the world, beginning with your organization.

* Leo Tolstoy, *Pamphlets* (translated from the Russian), Free Age Press, Maldon, Essex, 1900, p. 29.

ACKNOWLEDGMENTS

This book began as two books—one focused upon personal development and the other focused upon business development. Together there were seven hundred–plus pages of detail evidencing my own efforts to cross the divide between the habit of academic writing and the new goal of writing something for a general audience where the powerful message of the Seven Arts could be shared clearly and accurately. Based upon my initial efforts, I give myself low marks, to be sure! Without the brilliance and extraordinary talent of writer-editor Brent J. Cole, a master of the art of "putting yourself in the place of your partner," this book would not have taken its present shape. Thank you everyone for the causal stream of connections specifically related to this book project. It goes like this . . . Soshu Master Koichi Tohei, to Master Businessmen Jack Goldsmith, Bob Kidder, Charlie Perrin, Charlie Kiernan, Dave Bluestein, Moe Mayrant, Larry Hillard, Larry Ware, Ed Battocchio, Bob Correll, Nevin Caldwell, Terry Copeland, Harry Taylor, Paul Cheeseman, Mike Garris, Stan Brant, Rick Kerrigan, and Frank Santora who believed deeply in Bob's "Nine Great Investments" where people, products, and quality of life mattered *strategically*, to Judith Alexander, to Eric and Christina Harrell, to Belinda Hilliard and Evelyn Onofrio, to Greg Gardner, to Mark Stone, to Gloria Karpinsky, to Cheryl Woodruff, to Don and Gary Brozek, to Ryan Fischer-Harbage, to Philip Turner, to the team at Sterling Publishing, including Editor Iris Blasi, Editor-in-Chief Michael Fragnito, Publisher Jason Prince, and President Marcus E. Leaver. Thank you for your kindness, support, and understanding of the transformational power of the Seven Arts process.

INDEX

ABOUT THE AUTHOR

David Edward Shaner is the Herring Professor of Asian Studies and Philosophy at Furman University, where he has taught for the last twenty-nine years. Dr. Shaner has also taught at Harvard University when he was awarded an Andrew W. Mellon Faculty Fellowship in the Humanities–Department of East Asian Languages and Civilizations. He is the author of *The Bodymind Experience in Japanese Buddhism* (SUNY Press) and a co-author of *Science and Comparative Philosophy* (E. J. Brill) with Shigenori Nagatomo and YUASA Yasuo. Dr. Shaner is also the founding editor of the "Philosophy and Biology" book series (thirty-seven volumes) with the State University of New York Press.

David Shaner is also a former collegiate and Olympic Valley USA ski racer, former Deputy Sheriff law enforcement officer in Aspen, Colorado, and occasional trainer of world champion and national champion athletes and musicians for the past twenty-five years.

Dr. Shaner has been a Fulbright Scholar in India and has received numerous grants from the National Endowment of the Humanities and the National Science Foundation. He is a "Crown Prince Akihito Scholar" and was granted a personal audience with His Majesty, Emperor Akihito (Japan).

For forty years, Dr. Shaner has been a student of Master Koichi Tohei, founder of *Shinshin Toitsu Aikido* and the International *Ki* Society. Today Shaner *Sensei* holds the *Ki–Aikido* rank of *Nanadan* (Seventh Degree Black Belt), holds the rank of *Okuden* in *Ki* Development, and he is an Authorized Special Examiner and Chief Instructor of the Eastern (United States) *Ki* Federation, a branch of *Ki no Kenkyukai*, International. Shaner Sensei is also Japan Headquarters' Advisor to the Eastern Europe/Russia *Ki-Aikido* Federation.

For over twenty years, Dr. Shaner was the Principal of Shaner & Associates: Performance Development Consultants. Shaner & Associates facilitated their corporate clients' ability to lead change and execute their business strategies and operational plans. Clients included Umbro, Frito-Lay, Duracell, Ryobi, Gillette, Owens Corning Composites, Synthetic Industries, and many others.

Today Dr. Shaner is the Principal of CONNECT Consulting, LLC which not only helps to create measurable and sustainable performance improvement for corporations, but also his consulting services are expanding to include non-profits, peak performance training for experienced athletes and musicians, as well as individual counseling for executives and leaders of all kinds who seek a committed Seven Arts approach to continuous performance improvement.

To learn more, see DavidShaner.com.